To *Light* a
Penny Candle

"Alex's Easter and Christmas sermons… are beautifully written. The man has a bit of the poet in him and [his writing] tells of his deep passion and compassion. This book is a gift and a treasure." -Eveline Goodall

"Alex is a poet of deep faith… He is a master weaver of the story, drawing on the hundreds of threads from early childhood in his beloved Scotland. One is drawn into his well-crafted message which never fails to leave the listener with a sense of hope, with renewed affirmation of the strength of the human spirit…" -Rev. Dr. Bruce and June McIntyre

"Abandon any concept of being 'preached to' or sermonized in a manner that leaves you feeling small or inadequate. Rev. Lawson has a knack for expressing God's Love such that readers or hearers feel expanded in both heart and mind. His messages apply to daily life, are full of his trust, zest and Joy in God, and are always delivered with lyrical beauty. We are moved and inspired, wrapped in Grace, and Love, and left desiring to fully live the Teachings of Jesus. His Christmas sermons shine a Light into the darkest time of year and will keep the Path lit the whole year through." -Bryan and Barbara Huston.

"For the past twenty years Rev. Dr. Alex Lawson has been a key spiritual leader and mentor in the Waterton community. His clear and welcoming theology is based upon the integration of healing theories and the unconditional love of Christ. These sermons are gems which inspire and lift the heart of those who hear or read them." -Carol Watt, Chairperson of the Board, Waterton United Church

"Alex Lawson has a way of touching souls, lifting spirits and bringing scripture alive. He blends eloquence with humor; his sermons inspire me to feel better about myself and my fellow man. I aspire to be a better Christian through his ministry." -Maxine Reidell, Psychotherapist

To *Light* a Penny Candle

Rev. Dr. Alex Lawson

Order this book online at www.trafford.com
or email orders@trafford.com

Most Trafford titles are also available at major online book retailers.

Lethbridge, Alberta
Edited by Sandy Lawson

Printed in the United States of America.

ISBN: 978-1-4269-9485-2 (sc)
ISBN: 978-1-4269-9486-9 (e)

Trafford rev. 09/16/2011

www.trafford.com
North America & International
toll-free: 1 888 232 4444 (USA & Canada)
phone: 250 383 6864 ♦ fax: 812 355 4082

To Dr. Jack and Wendy Sherman, with fondness. The light of their love has shone every corner of my life.

Foreword

The Reverend Dr. Alex Lawson preached at McKillop United Church in Lethbridge, Alberta, from 1978 to 1991. It was his fifth, his longest, and his final full-time pastoral charge, though he has remained active in retirement. I recall the first sermon he gave at McKillop. Before beginning, he apologized for two shortcomings: a cold, which made him hoarse, and his Scottish accent. The cold, he assured us, would get better. Indeed, many found his dialect difficult at first, but when our ears became attuned to the lilt of his brogue, we began to relish it as an integral part of his sermons, just as we appreciated the twinkle in his eye when he grasped our hands as we filed past him out of the church, or the sad strains of the bagpipes, as, on Remembrance Sundays, Alex would stand in the narthex playing, "The Flowers of the Forest."

One aspect of Alex Lawson's reputation had preceded him. We had heard of him as a pioneer in the field of "Transactional Analysis," and the creator of the Family Life Education Centre, in the early 1970's, in Minto United Church, Moose Jaw, Saskatchewan. The largest in the province, it provided (and still provides, though in a new location) individual counseling and parent training, which are conducted by both professionals and lay-leaders, that is people who have participated in a program as a student, then volunteered to pass on to the next class the things they have learned. This was Alex Lawson's practical response to the great mystery of human misery, rooted in his belief that you can "love people into wholeness," by helping them to find the good in themselves. This belief has informed his long and loving ministry.

Alex Lawson came from humble beginnings in Scotland, and in his early years worked as a coal miner and a blacksmith's helper, even a common labourer. However, the poetry in his soul was revealed by his love for, and skill in playing, the bagpipes. The bands he taught and played with won many trophies. In 1950 he emigrated to Canada, where he furthered his education, (and his bagpipe playing!), finally graduating from McGill University with a degree in Theology. He was ordained by the United Church of Canada in 1963, and later awarded an Honorary Doctorate of Divinity by St. Stephen's College, Edmonton.

Yet Alex is still able to see life in the light of the tallow lamp worn by his coal-mining father. His sermons recall mining disasters, and even stories told to him by schoolteachers when he was just ten years old. But just as poignant are the glimpses he gives us of his adopted country of Canada: the plight of the immigrant families he first encountered when he worked as an installer for the Bell Telephone Company in Montreal; the death of his babysitter in a car-train collision one tragic night in Saskatchewan.

These are, for the most part, homespun sermons, preached to congregations of prairie folk; and they are usually topical, rather than exegetical. But they still manage to surprise and delight with flashes of insight, and wisdom; and to paint in memorable and often lyrical terms a picture of a loving God, as well as (by negative space, as it were) a portrait of his loving minister.

Shrewd observation of human behaviour has made Dr. Lawson an excellent psychologist. He first tackles the problem of denial, envisaging human problems as an elephant in a living-room: problems so big, so obvious, that people will not see them, accepting them as part of the normal condition of life. In the same way, he observes that "people will see what they expect to see. Their expectations will determine their conclusions. If they are looking for something to criticize, they will find it. If they are looking for something to appreciate, they will find it." But life doesn't have to be that way. People can change. He admires courage, and sees it in the man Jesus. He points out that it is not our basic make-up to be timid. "The human baby is born with great courage, but often the most well-meaning parents teach their children a multitude of fears." He addresses those who have become so accustomed to their slavery that liberty itself has become a threat. Though he concedes that we live in a scientific age, where rationalist thought prevails, he constantly reminds us that there is more to reality than meets the eye. He understands our common doubts as to whether the great Creator of the infinite universe could really care about us, but quells them instantly by reminding us to consider not only what is revealed by the telescope but also the microscope. The Designer was as careful over the minutest detail on earth, as He was over the vastness of space. He confesses he hates to throw things away, and rejoices that God doesn't discard anyone as worthless. He dismisses "vain regrets," preferring to look ahead than to dwell on mistakes of the past. He reminds us that we cannot help those whom we don't respect (a brilliant thought), and tells us that we must accept all of God's children. Unconditional love is the answer.

To read these sermons, particularly the Christmas ones, is to feel a quickening of hope, a renewal of faith in the grand design, and a deeper love for the Designer. Dr. Lawson's own appreciation of life and his fellow-man and woman is found in every line. He himself receives great inspiration from his own frequent trips to the Holy Land, finding great truths in small events. For example, archaeological work near the Church of the Cock-Crow, where, traditionally, it was believed that Jesus was held on the night of his arrest in the Garden of Gethsemane, has revealed a courtyard "right where the Bible said it would be," and beside it a flight of stairs. "And a shiver goes through me. This place has a ring of authenticity: those are the steps that Jesus ascended, this is the courtyard where people warmed themselves by the fire, this is the place where Peter heard the Clarion of the dawn."

Sermons are always worth reading; but inevitably, as they are performance pieces, they can look a little flat upon the printed page. The sermons of Laurence Sterne, for example, are--we might think--too dull to have come from the pen that created *Tristram Shandy*. So the sermons in this book, readable and powerful though they are, do not do justice to their effect when delivered from the pulpit by Alex himself. While they reveal something of his strong and vibrant personality, his concern for justice and fairness, and his wide reading, they cannot give the full force of his passion and warmth, or his ready sense of humour. Moreover, as a speaker who thinks on his feet, he is prone to taking the odd delightful detour during his preaching. The printed page can only hint at that. But, since the art of the preacher, like that of the actor, is evanescent, we are grateful that these sermons have been written down, and are finally to see the light of print, to "keep back Beauty," in Hopkins's words. To try and give permanence to the ephemeral. Or, as was well said by the eighteenth century Puritan, George Swinnock, "Sermons preached, or men's words, pass away with many like wind—how soon are they buried in the grave of oblivion! But sermons printed are men's works, live when they are dead, and become an image of eternity: 'This shall be written for the generation to come.' "

I feel sure that coming generations will be delighted to keep a copy of Dr. Lawson's sermons on their bedside table, to dip into on winter nights, for warmth, comfort and inspiration.

~Brian Tyson, Professor Emeritus of English Literature, University of Lethbridge

Introduction

When I started in ministry preaching was a frightening business but as the years went by it was an exhilarating experience. I loved it. My week built up to that moment when I joined the choir for the Processional at the opening of worship. In a very busy church with a vast array of programs, several of which I led, most of my sermons were written at one sitting on Saturdays between weddings (I had 83 in one year). On Tuesday my secretary would stop me in mid stride and ask for a sermon title for the paper and I would come up with a title and often wondered why but I came to trust my utterances – if I said the words it meant that there was a sermon within me.

Preaching is never done in a vacuum. A sermon has its origin in the congregation, is preached for the congregation and the responses of the congregation are all important. Some of those folks whose comments endeared them to me – Bill Clark, who would say, "Get that one printed; I'll pay for it", Big Bob Dunn and Ethel, Roger and Bea Meintzer, Sheila Matson, Maxine Reidel were always supportive. Dr. Bob Anderson commented that I was "all of a piece." Dr. Brian Tyson said of my sermons that they stimulated his thinking, nurtured him and made him laugh. Roy Hamilton, a renowned physician, who used my writings for his devotionals; Eveline Goodall and Noel Rea in St. David's, Calgary; Lois Jacobson and Joan Graham in Bow Slope and my dear friend Dale, the patriarch of the Patterson clan in Rolling Hills, were always supportive and very appreciative of my sermons.

This is a collection of my Christmas and Easter sermons. I usually sent a sermon with my Christmas greeting and many of you encouraged me to publish them. Famous author, psychotherapist and minister,

Muriel James, wrote. "…the sermons you sent me touch me at a deep level and they also light up the sky and world once more. Thank you, thank you, Alex… You have a remarkable talent with words. I hope one day you publish a book, 'Sermons from a Bagpiper'. People need to hear your message."

I have always taken preaching seriously. When I was at McGill, regardless of the pressure, I would run down to St. James United Church to hear renowned orators and I have studied the sermons of great preachers.

Preaching is a much less demanding medium forum than writing and thus I kept no footnotes. The influences of others are appreciated.

These sermons were preached in the context of music with the cooperation of a choir and organist and I want to thank my fine organists for their support over the years: Marilyn Sinclair, Carol Watt, Jackie Sereda, Carmen Graham and Douglas Hales.

I love the colour and drama and music of the Christmas story and the events of Easter. On Christmas Eve I use my electrical skills to flood the church with warm light and create a manger scene aglow with numerous candles. My goal is that any child attending would always remember church on Christmas Eve. My hope is that these sermons will have the same effect on the reader and I hope you will hear echoing through my every Christmas Eve, the hauntingly beautiful voice of Barbara Hamm singing "O Holy Night".

All these sermons were written to be preached and the reader will get the most out of them if they are read aloud.

~Alex Lawson, Lethbridge, Alberta

A God Who Visits

It was a terrible way to start the New Year. It was one of those times we talk about years later and ask, "*Where were you when...*"? It was over half a century ago in Scotland...

I was sitting in our local picture house when the work horn sounded and the urgency of its continuing blasts told me that there was trouble in one of the pits. An explosion in Burngrange, the pit at the top end of our village. One man was dead and fourteen were trapped behind a heavy fall of roof and the roaring flames of burning shale. The whole village, it seemed, gathered at the pit head to watch the drama.

As the days passed hopes faded, then miners, aided by fire fighters, got through to recover the fourteen bodies. There was hardly a family in our small community untouched by the disaster. The boy next door to us had previously been carried out of that same pit with his leg so badly smashed it had to be amputated. His mother gave thanks to God that her son could no longer go down the pit and was spared. Such is life in a mining village.

Later that week I stood by the graveside and listened to the minister's words, which drifted to me over the crowd of mourners. In the background smoke rose lazily from the shaft of the still burning pit. It is a scene still etched in my mind these many years later.

A clergyman, seeking to comfort the stunned community, used a prayer of his Church which asked God to:

> "*Bow down Thine ear in pity unto Thy servants, upon whom Thou hast laid this heavy burden of sorrow. Teach them*

to see Thy good and gracious purpose working in all the trials which Thou dost send upon them..."

There is a plaque in a coal mining village near Manchester, England, commemorating a mining disaster. It reads, *"In the year 1823, the Lord terribly visited the colliery of Robert Clark and the following were called to meet their Maker"*; there follows a list of twenty-three names.

It appalls me to hear anyone describe such a disaster as a "visitation of the Lord". But it is even more appalling to learn that every one of the twenty-three who died in the disaster was under nine years of age.

A "visitation" of the Lord is how we are supposed to view disaster and tragedy according to this type of theology. But as a miner become minister, I would never stand at a pit head and attribute the ongoing disasters that befall miners as "visitations from God". I knew all too well that it was the greed of the owners, who lived in mansions and owned vast estates, and the stupidity of subservient management, who turned a blind eye to obvious hazards that maimed and killed miners with great regularity.

It was commonly believed that to make a mine safe would price coal out of the market, and so it proved to be when the British pits were nationalized and most were closed. I am sure that if child labour laws were not enacted, we would still have the slaughter of children today and foolish clergy talking about the will of God. I wonder how many have turned away from the Christian faith because of this perverse belief about the nature of God.

Jesus came to counter this kind of thinking. God, he teaches us, is a healer not a killer:

"It is not the will of my Father that one of these little ones should perish", said Jesus. ~Matthew 18:14

Jesus came to teach us the true nature of God, and the word he uses to do so is the Aramaic, "Abba"; which is a child's word for his father. It is usually translated as "Father", but some theologians and linguists think it would be more accurately translated as "Daddy".

When Jesus, in the "Sermon on the Mount", wants to impress upon his cautious and fearful followers the nature of the Father to whom he is introducing them, he says:

"Is there a man among you who will offer his son a stone when he asks for bread, or a snake when he asks for fish? If you, then, bad as you are, know how to give your children what is good for them, how much more will your heavenly Father give good things to those who ask him?" ~Matthew 7:9 - 11

One of the characteristics of the Christian God that separates him from all other deities is that 'He' is a visitor. Folks of other faiths may go to holy places to visit their gods but not the Christian. Ours is a God who comes to us.

The season of Advent is all about God's coming to his people. The Christian God is a visitor. The main thrust of the Christmas story is that God, the great Creator God of the whole universe, has come to earth to live among his people. But the true wonder of it all - the tremendous revelation of that first Christmas - is that love came down to be among us and revealed to us God's true nature.

People were afraid to meet God until that starry night when he descended the stairway of eternity to reveal himself as he truly is to humankind. When they saw him they were amazed, for he came in the form of a helpless child.

No wonder they were taken aback, for the God we find in the history of the Hebrews is often a vindictive God; a cruel God, a God of earthquake and fire, a God of judgment and retribution, a God of slaughter and vengeance, and a God who at times sent plagues and pestilence, sickness and disease, and famine and starvation. He is portrayed as a God whose will was seen in the slaughter of infants and the annihilation of non-Israelites.

In fact one would be justified in thinking that it would be better for all concerned if God were to stay in heaven, for if he were to appear on earth we - like Adam and Eve - would be tempted to go into hiding rather than be found by him. But, wonder of wonders, when, in the fullness of time, God did choose to reveal himself to men and women, he came, not only with the humble and helpless to dwell, but humble and helpless to be.

As Walt Whitman has so eloquently put it in some of my favourite words about Christmas:

"He is not standing afar off waiting for us to draw nigh,
but a God who sought us out,
striving ever to enter, trying doors, strategically planning,
making himself as small as a child and lying down on the
doorstep of the world.

The world, moved by the cry of a child,
stealthily opened a door that had remained barred
against the thundering tempest and avenging words, took
the child in and unwittingly let God through."

No longer need humankind be afraid of a God who visits his people. For: God is love, and he who lives in love lives in God, and God lives in him. O, come to my heart, Lord Jesus, there is room in my heart for you.

The Dustman Cometh

"The angels keep their ancient places; -
Turn but a stone and start a wing!
Tis you, yis your stranged faces,
That miss the many splendoured thing. "
~Francis Tompson

"What did you go out in the wilderness to see? A reed shapen by the wind?" ~Luke 7:24

The coming of royalty usually means a time of preparation. I remember when the Queen came to Montreal, Quebec. I was a piper with the Black Watch and we spent months of spit and polish to prepare for her coming.

When the day finally arrived we were to parade at the Chalet on Mount Royal where she was to have lunch. We waited for hours but when her carriage approached, we were moved into the lane behind the Chalet and the Queen passed so quickly she didn't even see us.

It reminded me of a time when I was a boy in Scotland when we lined the railway embankment to watch the Royal Train go by. We thought that the train would stop or slow up but it thundered past with ne'er a glimpse of the Queen. Even the pennies we put on the rails to have the Royal Train flatten were never found again.

In Montreal, we did get to play for the troops while the Queen was at lunch with the dignitaries. But, again, when she was due to come out we were shunted back around to our place beside the garbage cans.

However, she must have heard us play because when she spotted us, she turned to Prince Philip and said something to him and pointed at us before disappearing. When we were dismissed, Jock Collie, an old piper in the front rank, turned to the rest of us and said, "Did you hear what the Queen said to Philip? She said, 'There's Jock Collie!' ".

There is that moment that breaks the tension whenever there is a ceremonial parade involving horses in the streets of London. It is the time when after long hours of waiting, some of them from the night before, when the chattering crowds are hushed in expectation as the appointed time for the royal coach draws near. The route has been cleared, the Bobbies are in position and the Horse Guards have been drawn up. The television cameras are in place, the commentators are at the ready, then along comes the Dustman with his barrow and brushes, cleaning up the last bit of mess before the Queen comes. Usually in the nature of the Londoners someone calls for three cheers for the Dustman and with mock dignity he doffs his cap to the crowd. And so the Dustman cometh, preparing the way for the arrival of the monarch. It is an absurd, yet essential part of the pageantry.

To the crowds who had gone out to the wilderness, people who had been waiting not hours or days, but years - centuries even, for the coming of the Messiah, the sight of John the Baptist suddenly emerging from the wilderness with his coat of camel hair and girdle of leather eating locusts and wild honey must have taken them aback. The Book of Leviticus, with its myriad of food laws, isn't big on craw dads or pig's feet, but the locust - be it the great locust, the long-headed locust, the green locust or every kind of desert locust - is on the recommended list and may be scoffed at will.

In any case, the sight of him, the first health food nut, munching on his locusts and dipping them in honey, must have seemed to them quite as incongruous as the arrival of the dustman doffing his hat ahead of the royal procession. Here was a man: a wild man, rough, uncouth and unknown, announcing himself as the Herald of the Lord, the forerunner of the Messiah.

It is obvious from the scriptures that they weren't impressed; they thought that God could have chosen someone more suited for the task. But Jesus took them to task saying,

"What did you go out in the wilderness to see? A reed shaken by the wind? A man dressed in silks and satins? Surely you must look in palaces for grand clothes and luxury. But, what did you go out to see? A prophet? Yes indeed. ~Luke 7:24 - 26

Then Jesus says accusingly,

"Today's generation are like children in the marketplace shouting at each other, 'We piped for you and you would not dance. We wept and wailed, and you would not mourn' ". ~Luke 7:32

"John the Baptist came neither eating bread nor drinking wine, and you say he is possessed, The Son of Man came eating and drinking and you say he is a glutton and a drinker". ~Luke 7:33 - 34

For many people, John didn't fit the part, but for others - the crowds who came to be baptized - he pointed to a new day: the Advent of the lord.

The New English Bible catches the mood of the crowd beautifully, like the crowds waiting for royalty. They are on "tiptoe of expectation". What better words to describe Advent to those who wanted to know what was required of them in this time of preparation than "on the tiptoe of expectation". To this day the Jews have elaborate ceremonies in preparation for the coming of the Messiah.

John replied:

"Take care of one another. Those who have are to give to those who have not."

It was a social gospel and those who repented would be known by their fruits. He also told them to clean up their act. The Tax collectors were not to cheat and the soldiers were not to blackmail. In other words, they were to serve God and each other in the workplace. Here they would show the fruits of their repentance. Let the tax collector be a good tax collector, Let the soldier be a good soldier.

"Prepare a way for the Lord" is the call of John to all who would, at this Advent season, be standing on tiptoe of expectation for the coming of the Lord. Repent. Share with those who are less fortunate than yourselves; be honest in your dealings with others and let your lifestyle show in the workplace, the office, the field, the home, the classroom, the factory and the supermarket - wherever you spend your days and interact with others. Love one another as God in Christ loves you.

Advent is a time of preparation. It is a time when we prepare for the coming of the Son of God who has no home, no dwelling place but the human heart… and there can be no room there if it is filled with bitterness, anxiety, shame, anger or judgment. All these must be displaced to make room for love and the coming of the Lord. For as in the beginning, He comes with the lowly and humble to dwell and will make a Bethlehem of our hearts.

This is the wonder and glory of the Christmas story:

Anyone can be a herald of the Lord and a spokesperson of his coming;

anyone can be a forerunner preparing the way of the Lord;
anyone can offer a humble abode for the mother of the Child;
anyone can welcome the Child and lay gifts at his feet;
anyone can walk with the Lord and be his humble servant; and,
anyone can embody the Christ and be an instrument of God's love in our world.

There is an old black spiritual that goes like this:
"There's a king and captain high,
And he's coming by and by,
And he'll find me hoeing' cotton when he comes.
There's a man they thrust aside
Who was tortured till he died,
And he'll find me hoeing' cotton when he comes.

He was hated and rejected,
He was scorned and crucified,
And he'll find me hoeing cotton when he comes.
When he comes? When he comes
He'll be crowned by saints and angels when he comes.
They'll be shouting out Hosanna! to the man that men denied,
And I'll kneel among my cotton when he comes."

John was forerunner of Jesus, a clearer of the way. A humble servant, unfit he said, to untie his sandals. A dustman clearing the way for the Royal procession, he calls all of us, whoever we are, and whatever our station in life to do our part to prepare the way for the coming of the Lord.

Great Expectations

"Thou art coming to a King,
Great expectations with thee bring"
~George Herbert , "The Church Porch"

There's a store in Montreal I used to pass on my way to work which had the intriguing name, "Great Expectations". It featured maternity dresses and everything else associated with expectant mothers and their babies. Great expectations indeed! What a grand name! What a wonderful way to describe a particular time of life - and what a wonderful attitude to have toward all of life.

Great expectations.

We are now into the season of Advent,

a time of expectation;

a time of anticipation;

a time of preparation;

a time when, as one translation of the bible puts it, the whole world stands on tiptoe to see this amazing thing that has happen and continues to happen wherever men, women and children seek to welcome the Christ Child into their lives.

We are waiting for a happening and, if we are prepared, it will happen. But… if our expectations are too low; if Christmas looms up as something to survive because of all the extra work, the multifarious activities, things to make and things to do, and no time to do them, then we will miss the wonder and glory of it all.

Each week I put in our bulletin a section called "A moment for quiet reflection." It is usually some poem or a bit of prose that reflects some aspect of the theme of our worship.

The one I didn't put in this week was:

"... 'Pussy Cat, Pussy Cat, where have you been?'
'I've been up to London to see the Queen!'
'Pussy Cat, Pussy Cat, What did you there?'
'I frightened a little mouse under her chair'... "

I can imagine how all the cats in cat-town gathered in preparation for this adventurous cat's trip to London to see Her Royal Majesty the Queen, no less. All the neighbourhood cats would be there: alley cats, house cats, tabby cats, fat cats, hungry cats, calico cats, exotic cats and even barn cats all the way in from the farm. All gathered to see her off on this momentous occasion. What excitement would fill the air.

And upon her return, what a gathering there would be, as they waited with anticipation to hear about all the wonders she had seen. "Pussy cat, Pussy cat, what did you there?" You can imagine the let down and their acute disappointment when she replied, "I frightened a mouse under her chair". Heck, she could have stayed home and done that.

Some years ago a group of my piping friends in Montreal, who were members of the R.C.A.F Pipe Band, flew over to Scotland to participate in the World Pipe Band Championships held that year in Edinburgh. I expected that being stationed on the outskirts of the town, and having lots of spare time, they would see a great deal of that royal city so steeped in history - and so dear to my heart.

I asked them on their return if they had enjoyed Edinburgh...

Had they visited the castle standing guard over the city as it has for a thousand years?

Had they seen there, the crown jewels of Scotland: the crown, the scepter and the sword?

Had they viewed Princes Street and the Gardens from the top of Sir Walter Scott's monument - and seen the Kingdom of Fife across the grey waters of the Firth of Forth?

Had they visited the ancient Cathedral of St. Giles, the High Kirk of Edinburgh, and seen the pulpit from which John Know, the great reformer, had thundered forth preaching defiance at Mary Queen of Scots and her monstrous regiment of women?

Had the seen the statue of Greyfriar's Bobby, the faithful wee dog, who wouldn't leave his masters grave?

Had they traveled the Royal Mile from the Castle to Holyrood Palace and viewed the spot where Rizzio, accused of being the Queen's lover, was slain by the nobles of the land?

Had they seen the closes off the high street where Burke and Hare plied their body snatching trade and the drawing rooms where Rabbie Burns, the plowman poet, was the wonder of all the world?

No!

No, they hadn't done any of these things… But, they had been in every pub on Rose Street, from the poshest to the sleaziest. They had followed the instructions contained in the advertising of the beer and whisky makers; Johnny Walker had been their lighthearted companion. They got Younger every day and had Bell's Black and White before they left. They had expected to find Scotland a drinking man's country and that was the picture of Scotland with which they returned. Like the cat that went to see the Queen, they could have stayed home and done the same.

At the beginning of the season we now call Advent, John the Baptist came out of the shimmering wilderness of the Judean Hills to announce that the Messiah was coming.

He must have cut a strange figure, this wild looking character in the garb of the ancient prophet, with his camel skin coat and flowing beard.

Some of the townspeople who made the journey to see him were obviously taken aback at the sight of him and Jesus takes them to task. *"What did you go out in the wilderness to see?"* He asks, *"A reed shaken by the wind? A man clothed in soft raiment? Or did you go to see a prophet?"*

Jesus knows there is no winning with those whose minds are made and who are determined to judge others by their standards. John had come out of the desert in the garb of the ancient prophet, the personification of the aesthetic. He was the original health food nut, dipping his locusts into wild honey, and otherwise fasting while shunning wine. They called him a madman.

Jesus came mixing with all kinds of people, eating junk food and drinking wine. They said he was a glutton, a party-goer and the friend of riff raff and the common folk.

The truth is that people will see what they expect to see. Their expectations will determine their conclusions. If they are looking for something to criticize, they will find it. If they are looking for something to appreciate, they will find it.

Jesus, we remember, could not do any good work in the face of a critical audience. Even He was rendered impotent when confronted by those who had a low opinion of him. Those who expected Jesus to be no more than the carpenter's son saw just that. But those who recognized him as the Messiah experienced redemption and new life.

Often we will hear folks say, "I'll believe it when I see it", but Marshall Macluan has pointed out, *the truth is, I wouldn't have seen it if I hadn't believed it..."*

We see what we expect to see.

In his biography of the eminent judge Samuel Lebowich, Quentin Reynolds, the great World War 11 correspondent, recalls that when Judge Lebowich retired there was large gathering of his peers: Judges, lawyers, Police Chiefs, Public Defenders had come to honour him.

One asked, *"When a crime happens the first thing we ask is, "Did anyone see it", but in your courtroom you give little credence to eye witnesses. Why is that?"*

It was a time when most men smoked and the popular cigarette was Camel. Judge Lebowich said that most of them had a cigarette pack in their hands umpteen times a day, and he asked them to vote on the position of the Arab in the picture on every pack.

"Is the Arab sitting on the camel or leading it? He asked.

After the vote he told them to look at the picture.

"There is no Arab. You believed there was one only because I suggested there was one and you saw what you expected to see"

In an issue of "The Script", the newsletter of the International Transactional Analysis Association, Sam A. Lloyd quotes studies to illustrate how expectations affect performance: Douglas McGregor, in 1960, discovered that the primary factor in managers having good results or bad results with people is the managers' own expectations. When managers expect people to be lazy, undependable, and dishonest and so on, they inevitably end up with employees who behave the way they expected them to behave. When managers expect people to be honest, achievement oriented, dependable and hard-working, they end up with employees who lived up to those expectations.

Rosenthal and his associates studied this same phenomenon in the classroom in 1968. Rosenthal and his group gave false information to teachers about students who were chosen at random. Teachers were led to believe that some students were smarter and more academically gifted than others. The teachers were asked to keep this false information to themselves, not to treat the students differently, and to make sure that all of the students in their classes were treated fairly. The researchers observed the classes each day to discover if the teacher's expectations would produce different results.

Once again the self-fulfilling prophecy did its work. Students whom the teachers believed to be the brightest scored significantly higher on the same standardized test that had been administered before the experiment. They also learned and remembered more of the material covered in the school term. Those students who, according to the original test results were not any smarter or gifted than the others, performed much more effectively because their teachers expected them to do so.

From their daily studies, these researchers also discovered how the expectations were being communicated. The teachers made eye contact with the "bright" students three times as often, they smiled at them more frequently, they used their names more consistently, they touched them more often and they called on them more.

When directing a question to one of the "slower" student's teachers waited an average of three seconds for a response before turning to another student for the answer. If the question was directed to a "bright" student teachers waited an average of seven seconds before turning to another student for the answer. The assumption seemed to be that the "bright" student would know the answer. The teachers' expectations based on false information had predictable results.

I heard on CBC radio a medical research scientist saying that he didn't want to get people's hopes up. What a terrible thing to say.

Getting people's hopes and expectations up are what can make drugs effective.

Blair Justice, in his magnificent book, <u>Who Gets Sick</u>, documents many studies to demonstrate the power of expectations. He says,

> *"If a patient's doctor is enthusiastic about a new drug he is giving the person, the effects are almost always greater than if the physician were neutral or negative toward the medicine".*

Expectations.

How they colour our perceptions. Researchers always have to allow for the Placebo effect. Patients who believe that they are being helped usually reflect their beliefs and skew the studies.

Sixteen pregnant nurses who were experiencing sickness were give medicine they were told would stop them from being sick. In fact, they were given an emetic which helps people to throw up. All sixteen nurses stopped being sick.

Expectations.

Yuri Grugarin came back from the first manned flight into space and reported that he had been to heaven and hadn't seen God. Young John Gillespie Magee of the Royal Canadian Air Force came back from his flight and wrote:

> *"I have slipped the surly bounds of earth*
> *And danced the skies on laughter-silvered wings;*
> *Sunward I've climbed and joined the tumbling mirth*
> *Of sun split cloud - and done a hundred things*
> *You have dreamed of - wheeled and soared and swung*
> *High in the sunlit silence. Hovering there,*
> *I've chased the shouting wings along and flung*
> *My eager craft through footless halls of air.*
> *Up, up the long delirious burning blue*
> *I've topped the windswept heights with easy grace,*
> *Where never lark or even eagle flew;*
> *And, while with silent, lifting mind I've trod*
> *The high untresspassed sanctity of space,*
> *Put out my hand and touched the face of God."*

There's an old story about an old man sitting by the roadside when a traveler came along and asked him what kind of people lived in that village ahead.

"What kind of people did you leave in the last village?" asked the old man.

"They were a bad bunch. Backstabbing, gossipers, cheats. I'm glad to be free of them", replied the traveler.

The old man said, *"I'm afraid that those are the kind of people you will find in the village ahead."*

Another traveler came down the road and asked the same question.

"What kind of people did you leave", asked the old man?

"They were wonderful people, kind, considerate, generous, I was sorry to leave them", said the second traveler.

"Go on ahead", said the old man." *You'll find the same kind of people ahead"*.

Expectations.

When you hear the sounds of Christmas expect that once again Jesus will be anew in you. O Come to my heart Lord Jesus, there is room in my heart for you.

The Colour of Christmas

*"My heart leaps up when I behold
a rainbow in the sky:
So it was when my life began;
So it is now I am a man;
So be it when I grow old,
Or let me die!
The Child is Father of the Man;
And I could wish my days to be
Bound each to each by natural piety."*
~William Wordsworth

A Toronto company claims to have the technology to turn black and white film into colour, an accomplishment welcomed by movie buffs who want to view the old classics in glorious Technicolor™

There's a hunger in all of us for colour. When the first televisions came on the market they were soon followed by sheets of plastic tinted green along the bottom, blue at the top, and orange in the middle, which when placed on the screen gave the illusion of colour.

I remember being asked when leading a workshop on dreams, *"Do people dream in colour?"* This seems a daft question because human beings were made for colour. God's world is a world of colour. It was only the limitations of early photographic technology that produced pictures of the world in black and white. We were made for colour.

Christmas is a time for colour. There's little room for black and white at this season of the year. Everywhere we look the colours of

Christmas meet the eye. If you are like me you regret the day the tree comes down and

> the pine cones,
>> the rosy apples
>>> the holly wreaths,
>>>> the coloured lights,
>>>>> the Christmas cards,
>>>>>> the shimmering tinsel and the festooning garlands are

packed away for another year and the house reverts back to its plain self.

> Christmas, a time when the plain,
>> the ordinary,
>>> the commonplace and
>>>> the everyday are not adequate.

People who throughout the year show little enthusiasm for the dogmas of Christianity,

> who have little or no involvement in the life of the Church,
> who demonstrate only passing interest in things religious,
> who appear to have little concern about life's meaning or purpose,
> who probe not at all the depths of their existence, and;
> who exhibit no interest in matters spiritual, are moved to mount

precarious aluminum ladders to reach eves troughs to mount spot lights, clamber along slippery roof tops in sub-zero weather to place plywood Santa Clauses and angels.

They are moved to struggle waist deep in snow in mountain passes in search of an adequate tree, work like Santa's elves stringing lights and running extension cords to tax their circuits to the limit, that they might participate in and add their quota of colour to this festival of lights and colour that heralds the coming of the one whose promise is that He has come to be the Light of the world, to light up our lives and give us life, not plain, common or ordinary life, but life in all its fullness. Life shot through with meaning, purpose, joy and excitement, and the abundant life of His discipleship.

Could it be that, in the multifarious activities promulgate the Christmas season, there is an underlying hunger - a hunger which lies dormant most of the year like a bulb responding to warmth and light pushes its green shoots out of the darkness through the hard earth in its quest for life? A hunger that stirs within us; unsettling us, disrupting us and turns our face toward the light of Him in whom beauty and truth shone, who is the Light of the world.

Could it be that the activities of Christmas,
    the spirit of giving,
      the concern for the poor,
        the gathering of families,
          the attendance at church,
            the reaching out to others,
              the resurgence of tradition,
                the heightened compassion, and
                  the colour and music of Christmas, are signs of a hunger?

A longing and a yearning which is deeper than nostalgia and more of a racial memory for lost excellence.

Could it be that like Adam and Eve, they are living East of Eden and hungering for Paradise Lost? A hunger, a lost ness or a discontentment of those who have known colour and are asked to settle for black and white?

Or, the hunger discerned by Milton when he was casting around, seeking a theme to fulfill his ambition to write an epic poem in his own native language and do for his own native England what Virgil had done for ancient Rome, and Tasso for Italy.

For forty two years he harboured this great idea and cast around looking for an adequate theme for his great work. He went through subject after subject until he settled on the Biblical theme of Paradise Lost. He would relate the story of Adam and Eve being expelled from their paradise, Eden, into a world of toil, pain and sweat.

Could it be that with Adam and Eve we stand east of Eden and hunger for that lost state of being of which our present life is but a shabby semblance, with shades of grey and brown where once was verdant green? Work, sweat, tears and pain where once was bliss; thorns, thistles and wild plants where once along the river banks the fruit trees and precious herbs were profusely in abundance?

We might be willing to settle for a prosaic existence, a drifting, shiftless, hum drum life bereft of meaning and purpose but God isn't. Continually he prods us, disturbing our complacency and unsettling our lethargy. He interrupts our frantic activities; he calls a halt to our futile pursuit with the Divine Discontent - and our hearts are restless 'til they find rest in him.

Christmas is for children. Children of all ages - and if we would discover the true wonder and meaning of it all, we will hear the words of Jesus:

> "Whoever does not receive the Kingdom of God like a child will not enter it." - Mark 10:5

Jesus had a special place in his heart for little children. When the Chief Priests and teachers of the law came to him in the temple, angry at the shouts of the children and demanding that he silence them, He refused, saying,

> "Have you not read; Out of the mouths of babes thou hast brought perfect peace?"- Matthew 21:16

And when the disciples scolded the mothers who were bringing their children to Jesus for his blessing, Jesus was angry and said to his disciples:

> "Let the children come to me. Do not stop them because the Kingdom of God belongs to such as these. Whoever does not receive the Kingdom of God like a child will never enter into it." -Mark 10:13 - 16

Jesus wasn't inviting his followers to stop acting like grown-ups and be childish. There's a big difference between being childlike and childish. The Apostle Paul said:

> "When I was a child I spoke like a child, I thought like a child, I reasoned like a child, when I became an adult I put away childish ways" -1 Corinthians 13: 11

I think we all know the difference between "childlike" and "childish" behaviour. There is little appealing in childish behaviour in a grown person, such as one who pouts if he doesn't get his own way, who uses temper tantrums to keep people frightened and obedient to his will, who uses anger to control others, whose envy ruins friendships, whose displays of jealousy have the intent of stunting another's growth and restricting their involvement with others, whose stream of complaints poisons the atmosphere, who uses illness and self-neglect to keep others concerned, anxious and attentive, or whose lack of responsibility invites others to carry more than their share of the load.

No, there is nothing endearing or attractive about childish behaviour and the Apostle Paul instructs us to be done with it, to put it behind us, to grow up and act responsibly and be accountable.

Of course, while as Christians we are called to be done with childish things, we have a responsibility to those who are being childish no matter what age they are. We are called not to judge - although the temptation is awfully strong - but criticism and judgment are totally ineffective in bringing about changes in behaviour. Indeed, if we do fall into the trap of being angry and start to condemn, berate, nag or judge others, we end up being childish ourselves.

We don't readily discern that those who adopt the role of critic, or those who are self-appointed as the moral and behavioral watch dogs of the rest of the citizens in the community are acting in a childish manner. Their authoritative stance, their dogmatic self-assurance, their self-righteous indignation, their positive, inflexible, confident, arrogant or vehement posturing would invite us to behold them as people of stature and substance but, the fact is, that none of the adjectives I have just listed would ever be used to describe a mature person.

These are the childish acting out of old, immature and early programmed learnings and prejudices. Never the less, this is not to say that the childish are without influence. While the Rev. Ian Paisley may appear to some of us to be a blustering buffoon, he nevertheless has a powerful influence and a large following. The childish capricious, suspicious, whims and fancies and rug biting behaviour of Hitler made him not one whit less dangerous.

There is a fascination in our society with childishness. Take a look at the appeal of the Soaps where integrity and maturity of character are rare qualities indeed. Irresponsibility, shallowness, superficiality, manipulation, uncontrolled emotions and immature behaviour are constantly paraded.

One could say that the goal of Christianity is to stop childish behaviour. Childishness robs us of the joy of living; it keeps us mean, miserable and small minded. It takes away our vitality and enthusiasm; it cheats us of life in all its fullness and it invites us to think that there is not enough bread to go around. We sometimes settle for half a loaf and feel cheated.

We see the world in black and white when our God created it in glorious Technicolor™.

A cable television technician was called to a home in answer to a complaint that the colour was missing from a television set. It wasn't the cable that was at fault; it was the set. It was a black and white television! Nothing was wrong with the transmission. It was the receiver that was at fault.

It is likewise for all of us. If the world is a drab place devoid of fun, excitement, meaning and purpose, we are out of sync with God's glorious creation and we need to be turned around. It isn't unusual for someone who has experienced new birth to see the world in a new light.

How often I have seen someone make a life-changing decision and feel the weight fall off her shoulders, and walk away with a lighter step - with new vision and seeing the world as a brighter place.

This Christmas, when you see the colours of the season, may you see them through the eyes of a child, with all the wonder and excitement, the joy and happiness as well as the anticipation and gratitude of the child in your midst.

And a little child shall lead them.

May your eyes be drawn to that source of all light; the Child of Bethlehem, Jesus Christ, the Light of the World.

God in Our Midst

"Dreams they are, but are they God's dreams?"
~unknown

"I have a dream."
~Martin Luther King

There is something wonderful about seeing a dream come to fruition. Especially if it is "God's Dream," as Archbishop Desmond Tutu entitled his book about the end of apartheid… and who could watch the outpouring of emotion at President Obama's inauguration and not hear, ringing down history, the words of Martin Luther King: "I have a dream". One of the most remarkable scenes in the Old Testament is the description of the dedication of the Temple of Solomon. It too was the fulfillment of an ancient dream.

The author of the 2nd Book of Chronicles gets caught up in the wonder and excitement of it all and takes many pages in scripture to describe it. This is a momentous day in the life of Israel. It is the culmination of many years of preparation. First of all by King David, whose dream it was that a fitting resting place for the Ark of the Covenant be built in Jerusalem. A dream, although fulfilled by his son King Solomon, was certainly a dream that went all the way back to the children of Israel wandering in the desert dreaming about the land of the promise. A place where all their weary wanderings will cease and they will no longer be nomads without a place to call their own. No longer eking out an existence in the barren wastes of Sinai, but a settled people living in the land promised to their fore bearers - a land flowing with milk and honey - a land of trees and precious metals, a land of figs and pomegranates.

This was the ancient dream sustained over the years by the presence of God in their midst. It was this dream and their particular relationship with God that separated this people from all others.

They were a covenant people and the basis for that covenant was contained in two tablets given to Moses the day he encountered God on the mountain in Sinai. The tablets were placed in the Ark and wherever the people went the ark was carried on long poles on the shoulders of the priests went with them symbolizing the presence of God in their midst. It went with them in all their weary wanderings in the desert; it went with them when they crossed the River Jordan and entered the Land of the Promise. It went with them in all their battles with the Canaanites and the dreaded Philistines and though it was captured once, it was still with them when David united the tribes of Israel and became their king.

Under David the tribes forsook their nomadic ways and settled the land. They built villages and cities in which to live but the Ark of the Covenant had no permanent home and was housed in a tent.

This troubled David so he launched an ambitious plan to build a Temple in Jerusalem for the ark. It was to be a fitting dwelling place for the Lord Most High. But David never saw the completion of his dream. It was left to his son to bring it to fruition and Solomon erected a splendid edifice.

The Bible tells us he ranged far and wide seeking the choicest timber and the best workmen, the most precious metal and the finest artificers. They worked day and night and gave generously of their substance to build and adorn it. The finished edifice was glorious to behold and there it sits on the top of Mount Moriah for the entire world to see.

The people of Israel assembled for the dedication ceremonies and when the 120 Priests blew their trumpets I'm sure they felt as proud as the people in this congregation felt when they completed this building. Now it was time for the dedication:

King Solomon mounts the raised platform erected in front of the Temple and kneeling before the people he raises his hands toward heaven and prays,

"O Lord God of Israel there is no God like Thee in heaven or on earth keeping covenant with Thy servants and showing them constant love…" ~ 2 Chronicles 6:14

What a marvelous moment in the lives of the people. There was the magnificent Temple and deep within is the Holy of Holies housing the Ark of the Covenant: "

> *…And when the assembled crowd sang with trumpets and symbols and other musical instruments in praise to the Lord, 'For he is good, for his steadfast love endures forever' the house of the Lord was filled with a cloud so that the priests could not stand to minister, for the glory of the Lord filled the house of God…"* ~2 Chronicles 5: 13 – 14.

It is in this setting, in the middle of the festivities, when the hearts of the people are bursting with joy, in the middle of the prayer of dedication that King Solomon has a moment of self-doubt and he interrupts his joyful prayer:

> *"…But, will God dwell indeed with man on earth? Behold heaven and the highest heaven cannot contain Thee how much less this house which I have built…"* ~2 Chronicles 6:18

Many of us have known this same moment of doubt. We may be secure in our faith then we stand out in the midst of these vast prairies and gaze at the overarching panorama of the night sky with its countless stars involving distances far beyond the capacity of our minds to understand and we wonder if the great creator God of this vast universe does indeed care for us.

One thing we can do at a time like this is to remind ourselves not only what the telescope reveals but what the microscope reveals. It is not only the heavens and the unimaginable distances that fill us with awe but the microscopic detail of the human body and its genes. Not only are the hairs on our head numbered, our genetic makeup also is unique. We examine the human body and the more we know they more we realize we don't know and yet will someday find out and understand.

Certainly God is the great architect and sustainer of this vast universe but he also the designer who lavishes his ingenuity on the minutest thing in his creation. It is well to remember that it is we humans, we who feel so insignificant, who invented and designed the telescope and the microscope and measured the results.

We are the plotters of the heavens and who create satellites of our own to photograph and explore the planets. No star ever knew that it was watched or photographed. No star was ever moved to give thanks to God for all his wonders and enjoyed his fellowship. Centuries ago a Psalmist wrote:

> *"When I look at your heavens, the work of your fingers, the moon and the stars that you have established; what are human beings that you are mindful of them, mortals that you care for them? Yet you have made them a little lower than God. And crowned them with glory and honour…"* ~ Psalm 8:3

What the Psalmist affirms is what God's people have discovered as they seek a relationship with God. It is that the great creator of this universe is near to each and every one of us.

As Paul said to the men of Athens at the Areopagus on Mars Hill so long ago:

> *"…Men of Athens, the God who made the world and everything in it and who is Lord of heaven and earth, does not live in shrines made by men. It is not because he lacks anything that he accepts service at men's hands, for he is himself the universal giver of life and breath and all else".*
>
> *He created every race he tells us, and the purpose is "they were to seek God, and if it might be, touch and find him…. He is not far from each one of us, for in him we live and move and have our being…"* ~Acts 17:22 - 28

But will God dwell indeed with man on earth?

The answer is on every page of the New Testament: God, the great creator God of the whole universe did indeed come down to earth to dwell with men and women and inhabit, not King Solomon's Temple but the poorest of dwellings. And although of David's line and kin to Solomon himself, his family of choice were poor folks and humble.

But the true wonder of it all, the tremendous revelation of the first Christmas, was that love came down to be among us. What a revelation! I know had I lived in that time I would have been flabbergasted to find God, the powerful and terrible God of the Old Testament revealing himself to humankind in the form of a helpless little child.

The God we encounter in the history of the Jews is often a vindictive God;

a God of earthquake and fire;

a God of judgment and retribution;

a God of slaughter and vengeance;

a God who at times sent plagues and pestilence, sickness and disease, famine and starvation;

a God whose will was seen in the slaughter of infants, and in the annihilation of non-Israelites;

a God who needed to be placated by temple sacrifice and the keeping of the law; and

a God greatly to be feared.

In fact, one would be justified in hoping that perhaps it would be better for all concerned if God were to stay in heaven for if he were to appear on earth, we, like Adam and Eve, would be tempted to go into hiding rather than be found by him. But wonder of wonders, when in the fullness of time God did choose to reveal Himself to men and women; he came not only with the humble and helpless to dwell but humble and helpless to be.

Shall God indeed dwell with men on earth?

"*Yes indeed!*" cry the gospel writers, but not to dwell in Solomon's Temple or any other edifice built by human hands, for God is Love and he came to inhabit the human heart.

As George MacDonald, The Scottish mystic writes:

> *"They all were looking for a king*
> *To slay their foes and lift them high;*
> *Thou camst, a little baby thing*

That made a woman cry.
O Son of Man, to right my lot
Naught but Thy presence can avail;
Yet on the road Thy wheels are not,
Nor on the sea Thy sail!
My why or how Thou wilt not heed,
But come Thou down Thine own secret stair,
That Thou mayst answer all my need
– Yea, every bygone prayer."

O Come to my heart Lord Jesus; there is room in my heart for Thee.

The Melody of the Future

"Hope is the melody of the future, faith is the dance to it"
~Ruben A. Alves

We live in a predictable world. A world that modern science is helping us to understand. If there is some mystery, some puzzle or something that doesn't make sense, we still know that there is an answer. All that remains is for us to ask the right question and we will find the answer.

We live in a rational world, and thank God we do, for how else could we fathom the mystery of our existence if underneath and throughout all of creation there were not laws governing and controlling every event and movement. Science is helping us to understand this vast universe in which we find ourselves and of which we are part.

We are children of a scientific age. Since our birth we have been programmed to be rational creatures - to think in terms of fact, logic and empirical evidence. If something happens there must be a reason for it; a cause or explanation. "Seeing is believing" is our motto; nothing ever happens simply by chance.

But in the midst of all the hustle and bustle of our involvement with this everyday world of ours, there comes a dawning, a realization, an awareness, that perhaps there is more to reality than meets the eye - that beyond the colours of the rainbow that we can see, from the red at one end of the spectrum to the violet at the other, there are the infra-reds and the ultra-violets, and out beyond them again there are unimaginable reaches of colour which we never see at all, but whose presence we can measure, and whose power is awesome.

And beyond and throughout this law abiding, predictable world of ours, there is a spiritual world, which we cannot see but whose existence we perceive with the inner eye, whose presence we sense with the receptive heart, whose purpose we discern with the sensitive mind.

It is the world of the poet, the mystic, the visionary, and at no time is this world so real as at Christmas.

Christmas is a time for poetry. For me, one of the joys of Christmas is:
  the poetry associated with it,
    the poetry expressing the greetings of friends on Christmas cards,
      the poetry set to the music of our carols,
        the poetry of the Christmas story itself,
          the maiden and the journey,
           the man and the donkey,
            the inn and the manger,
              the heavenly host and the shepherds,
               the baby and the star,
                 the wise men and their gifts; it's all sheer poetry.

Christmas - a time for poetry and artistry, a time when men who would claim not to have an artistic bone in their bodies, or a creative thought in their minds, nor a spiritual side to their personality transform ordinary houses into Arabian palaces far beyond the scope of Aladdin's lamp or Genie slave.

Christmas - a time for poetry for how else could one convey the wonder and thrall of it all?

McGill University had a magazine whose back page was devoted to articles under the heading, Plain Talk. Dean Stanley Bryce Frost, our professor of Old Testament studies, was asked to contribute to the December issue, an article about Christmas. I can still hear him muttering,

"How could anyone write about Christmas in 'plain' talk?"

How indeed? For every facet of the Christmas jewel gleams with magic and mystery, and even the most pragmatic of us; the hard-headed, the practical, the down-to-earth, the logical and the rational of us gets caught up in the wonder of it all, and we become dreamers too.

We look at this world; this strife-ridden, hunger-stricken, disease-infested, corruption-riddled, sordid and tottering old world of ours and see things, not as they are, but what by the grace of God they could be. And the hope that is symbolized in the birth of every child springs eternally fresh in our hearts.

It is then that we sense anew the bright new era ushered in by the birth of the Christ Child, and we see possibilities for humankind so often obscured in the hustle and bustle of our practical every day world, where things visible, tangible, sensual and audible obsess our thoughts, fill our eyes, and preoccupy our hearing.

I remember a plaintive song I heard one Christmas,

"If only we could have Christmas all the rest of the year".

The singer's sentiments were fine. I'm sure there are many who wish that the warmth and the gaiety, generosity and the gratitude, the music and the colour, the festivity and the laughter, the love and the sentiment, the caring for strangers, the solidarity of families, the acceptance of others and the giving of ourselves could be carried on through the whole year and not stashed away for another year along with the Christmas tree ornaments.

But while the singer's heart is in the right place, her theology isn't, for the living message portrayed in the song, and in the poetry, and in the drama of Christmas - focusing as it does on the great and generous gift of God's love embodied in his infant son - is that the love and acceptance of the great God and Father of us all is freely available to every generation, at any time, in any place and on any day.

In the words of James S. Stewart,

> *"Christmas stands for the tremendous fact that in Jesus the ultimate eternal reality, the ground of all existence whom men call God, struck down into history and broke through into the life of man. Behind Bethlehem is the throne of Heaven, behind all the natural poetry of Christmas - the power and pressure of the supernatural. This is the Lord's doing and it is marvelous in our eyes..."*

Men were afraid to meet God until that night of nights when he descended the stairway of eternity and revealed himself in human flesh. For the first time in all recorded history people saw with their own eyes that God was, above all else, a God of love. In the songs the angels sang, they heard the melody of the future and in the days to come they would dance to it.

It was a sad, tired, disillusioned and tottering old world that first heard the melody of the future. For some it was a fearful sound, for encounters with God in the past had conditioned them to cringe in his presence, but when they recovered from the initial shock they could indeed, "Fear not", for God - the great God of the whole created universe - had come to them. He had come not in thunder, nor in lightening, nor in pestilence or in earthquakes… but in the form of a helpless, little child.

For others the melody meant the end of an era; the end of their power over people. And when they heard the song, they sought to kill the child whose birth heralded this new age.

For yet others, they had become so accustomed to their slavery that liberty was a threat. In his marvelous, heart-rending poem, "The Prisoner of Chillon", Lord Byron tells how a freedom fighter became so accustomed to his cell that when his release came he was reluctant to leave it:

> "…At last men came to set me free;
> I asked not why, and recked not where:
> It was at length the same to me,
> Fettered or fetterless to be,
> I learned to love despair…..
> My very chains and I grew friends,
> So much a long communion tends
> To make us what we are."

I see this story being relived today. Many of us today are hemmed in, shackled and bound by our fears, our failures, our inadequacies and our insecurities. We can hear the melody of the future, the call to freedom, the song of the angels to "*fear not*" but we are afraid to dance to it.

We are afraid to change.

We may be terribly uncomfortable being the way we are; we may be experiencing great anxiety and even pain. But where we are is familiar.

We've been stuck here for a long time and the thought of change, even the promise of new life, scares us and we choose to stay where we are.

There are three ways in which people change:

- Trauma
- A religious experience
- Therapy

Unfortunately, all too often we choose trauma: a heart attack, the loss of a loved one, a narrow escape, an excruciating pain, a terrible fright, or the breakdown of a marriage.

But, it doesn't have to be.

Pain isn't the only impetus for change from a mode of living that is depression-filled or anxiety-riddled.

We can put our lives into the hands of the living God, and live our lives under his care and direction, doing so without fear. For in the birth of his son God is saying, "Fear not!" "Trust me!" In this stupendous act of God revealing Himself to us as He really is. Fear is replaced by joy, for when *the Lord of all being, throned afar* did appear in our midst it was in the form of a helpless little child.

What a surprise!

In the words of an old carol:

> *"Who is he in yonder stall*
> *At whose feet the shepherds fall?*
> *And the wonderful, unbelievable answer;*
> *"'Tis the Lord - the King of glory.*
> *'Tis the Lord - O wondrous story,*
> *At his feet the shepherds fall,*
> *Crown him, crown him, Lord of all"*

There is something wondrously generous about our God who showers upon the unworthy the gift of his love. This God, who squanders the substance of His love on the unworthy, who wantonly sows His seed on the paths and rocky hillsides, who goes the second mile, who gives His coat as well as His shirt and who runs to meet the prodigal son who slinks home hoping for a few crusts and is given a hero's welcome, a banquet, a robe for his shoulders and a ring on his finger.

Our God is a generous God. The pages of the Gospels are full of accounts of His generosity. When this happens to us, when we experience the love of God through the acceptance and caring of his people, we hear the melody of the future. We hear the song of God's acceptance of us as his children.

And when people hear the melody of the future - God's great promise of new life in a supportive fellowship where there is acceptance and love, and they are enabled to put aside their fears to see themselves as they truly are, with all their possibilities and potential - they do change and it is beautiful to behold.,

This Christmas season, as you sing the Christmas carols and hear the familiar words of the Christmas story, will you listen for the melody of the future?

Will you consider giving up the shackles that chain you to your lesser self?

Will you consider getting out of your rut, and to walk with God in new paths?

Will you consider becoming the person God created you to be; the person you always wanted to be, the person you always hoped you could be, and the person you already are?

For the Christian gospel goes beyond hope. By faith we become children of God.

For *"Hope is the melody of the future, Faith is to dance to it".*

Surprised by Joy

"Oh glory of the lighted mind
How dead I'd been, how dumb, how blind,
The station brook to my new eyes
Was bubbling out of paradise,
The waters rushing from the rain
Were singing Christ has risen again.
I dreamt all earthly creatures knelt,
From Rapture of the joy I felt."
~John Masefield.

There's a hunger at the heart of us that has haunted human kind since the dawning of the ages. It is a hunger that impels us to quest and seek though we know not what we lack. It is a hunger to which some dedicate their lives; their every waking hour to finding although - in the finding - there may be no keeping. It is a hunger which has sent folks questing to the ends of the earth even though sometimes their journey's end has been near its beginning.

It is a hunger that haunts, a craving that impels and an emptiness that calls; which, in the finding, fills life with meaning and purpose and joy. It's a craving, a seeking and a finding that has captivated the poet, the philosopher, the artist and the theologian, for it lies at the heart of human existence. It is only in the finding that we become aware of what we were seeking. More than that, there is, in the finding a sense of awe; a sense of wonder; and, a sense of amazement.

St. Augustine said of the questing, *"There's a God-shaped blank at the heart of every man, and our hearts are restless 'till the find rest in Thee".*

I visited once more this week, in my mind's eye, the beautiful Lake District of North-West England and climbed again the Fells with my brother. We were amongst countless English folks seeking respite from the cities there to look down on the Meres below.

This is the area made popular in the late 1700's by Wordsworth's "Guide to the Lake District" which brought tourists by the droves and still does today. You may know that Wordsworth for some years drifted aimlessly seeking some vocation, some avenue that would bring sense and meaning to life.

His father was a solicitor but he shrank from the law. Wordsworth deemed himself not good enough for the Church and events in France turned him away from soldiering. Then, after a long spell of depression and sore disappointment, he found what he had been lacking. "It was", he says, "Natures self":

> *"By all varieties of human love*
> *Assisted, led me back through opening day*
> *To those sweet counsels between heart and head*
> *Whence grew that genuine knowledge, fraught with peace*
> *Which, through the later sinkings of this cause,*
> *Hath still upheld me and upholds me now".*

This motif of hunger and fulfillment, despair and hope, seeking and finding is common to Wordsworth. As I stood later at Tintern Abbey, I thought of his words written there which reflect this finding:

> *"And I have felt*
> *A presence that disturbs me with the joy*
> *Of elevated thoughts; a sense sublime*
> *Of something far more deeply interfused,*
> *Whose dwelling is the light of setting suns,*
> *And the round ocean and the living air,*
> *And the blue sky, and in the mind of man:*
> *A motion and a spirit, that impels*
> *A thinking things, all objects of all thought,*
> *And rolls through all things".*

What a moment that is when we experience that presence, that motion, that spirit that impels all living things. When into our solitude, our despair, our helplessness, comes that moment of awareness...

that sense of the divine...

that in breaking of the spirit...

that time of realization and revelation...

that we are not alone...

that we have not been abandoned...

that we are not without worth...

that we are children of the living God, who in our time of need fulfills his promise that

*"I will not leave you comfortless, I will come to you". ~*John 14:18

We are surprised by joy.

We are amazed that God, the God of this whole create universe, would deem us worthy and bless us with his presence. Perhaps this is what Wordsworth is saying in what is probably the best known of his poems:

"I wondered lonely as a cloud
That floats on high o'er vales and hills,
When all at once I say a crowd,
A host of golden daffodils;
Beside the lake, beneath the trees,
Fluttering and dancing in the breeze.

Continuous as the stars that shine
And twinkle on the milky way,
They stretched in never ending line
Along the margin of a bay:
Ten thousand saw I at a glance,
Tossing their heads in sprightly dance.

The waves beside them danced; but they
Out did the sparkling waves in glee:
A poet could not but be gay,
In such a jocund company:

I gazed - and gazed - but little thought
What wealth the show to me had brought"

In these last two lines Wordsworth becomes aware that there is more to this experience than meets the eye. This happy sight has touched him deeply but it is only later that he realizes just how deeply.

Something like this happens to me when I visit Israel. I see places the names of which I have known since childhood: Nazareth, Galilee, Jerusalem, Jericho, Bethlehem, and I love them all. I enjoy the sights and sounds of the Holy Land and I hunger for them. But months, perhaps years, later following my visit - when I am writing a sermon along with the visual memory of some biblical scene - a spiritual insight surfaces of which I was unaware.

It is only then that I become aware of my spiritual depth. I have responded to the place I saw at a deeper level than I supposed and I become aware that I have more spiritual depth and awareness than I realized. This is true, I think, of all of us.

We are spiritual beings. Sometimes we are not aware of it until we see the daffodils; some scene, some event or some place...

We experience the Holy in the commonplace: the burning bush in a host of golden daffodils.

There are times when we discount the spiritual self of others. Occasionally, the young people choosing to be married in our church do not support or attend any church and we welcome them. I know of ministers who are not as gracious - who believe that these couples are just using the church because it is a nice setting and very photogenic, etc. They claim that these young people do not have a spiritual or religious bone in their body.

Instead I give these young couples I am to marry a booklet I have compiled and adapted that they can choose A, B, C, D or E in all the sections of the marriage service. They are free to change, add, or delete any part of it. I want it to be *their* wedding so that the words they choose will reflect their prayers, their thoughts, their hopes and their sentiments as they pledge themselves to one another.

When they return the completed booklet I am frequently impressed by the depth of spirituality reflected in their choices and it may be that they, in planning the most important event in their lives, have discovered their own spirituality in new and profound ways.

Similarly, when a couple who do not attend church request baptism for their baby, I sometimes hear disparaging remarks about them wanting "the baby done" and that they are simply following a social custom. Or, they believe there is magic in baptism that confers immunity from most anything. But I know that usually their request comes from deep spiritual sources within them that they cannot verbalize but which are compelling and powerful.

Very often their families have been baptizing their babies for centuries and the ritual is a racial memory. Indeed studies now show that people have cellular memories that show up in transplants, like the woman craving a motorbike ride for her fortieth birthday and not understanding it because it was so out of character, until she learned that donor of her transplant was a biker. All of us have deeper reasons than we understand.

Wordsworth, is his lovely poem about the host of golden daffodils goes on to record how it is only later that he realizes how deeply he has been moved by the experience:

> "...For oft, when on my couch I lie
> in vacant or in pensive mood,
> They flash upon that inward eye
> Which is the bliss of solitude;
>   And then my heart with pleasure fills,
> And dances with the daffodils..."

Centuries ago, at the dawning of our faith, a young man - a conniving, scheming scoundrel and a con man of the first order - was on the run far from home. When the day was far spent he lay down in a desolate, rock strewn valley with a stone for a pillow and dreamt. It was not the dream of a fugitive with his feet in molasses trying vainly to outrun his pursuers, but found himself in the presence of God. When he awoke it was with a great sense of awe and he exclaimed,

> "Surely the Lord is in this place and I knew it not, this
> - this barren valley, this desolate landscape, - this of all places

is none other than the house of God.' And he called that place
Beth el, meaning 'house of God' ". ~Genesis 28:19

Sometimes a light surprises the Christian as he sings, or a host of golden daffodils commands the lonely poet as he wanders, or the stairway to heaven appears to the fugitive of Bethel.

There is this amazing quality in the grace of God. We are surprised by joy. We can hardly believe our good fortune. This is so much better than we dreamed possible, so much more than we ever imagined, and, of course, it is, it is much more; much, much more than we can ever possibly deserve. That is the essential nature of grace.

It cannot be earned; it cannot be purchased; it cannot be deserved; it is a gift of God, freely given, and we are surprised by joy.

"Behold the amazing gift of love
the Father hath bestowed on us,
the sinful children of men and women
to call us children of God"
                                        ~Isaac Watts

I spoke with a woman of a different denomination whose son was marrying a Roman Catholic girl. The couple had chosen the United Church as neutral ground. The mother didn't want to light a candle that I usually have as the mother's light, she didn't have a way of getting to the rehearsal and she yet couldn't do it without a rehearsal. She complained her feet weren't good; they swelled up if she sat too long, but she had told her son she will show up at the wedding.

I could see that her reluctance, and indeed the swelling of her feet, was based on her deep disappointment that he wasn't getting married in her church. She's coming to the wedding but she is dragging her feet, she's acting out her reluctance and she's letting him know that she's going grudgingly.

I suggested to her that she surprise him by being enthusiastic, by supporting him in his choice of wife, by going the second mile and by being generous as God is generous. How easy it is to be truculent, to be stubborn, to pay him back, be uncooperative, and to show him how disappointed we are...

But how wonderful it is when we meet folks who put aside their hurt feelings and go the second mile. Those who give us more than we would dare to ask for, gracious friends that are there to support us no matter what. This is what Jesus meant when he said:

"If a man asks for your shirt, give him your coat. If a soldier asks you to carry your pack one mile (which was the Roman law) *carry it another mile..."* ~ Matthew 5:40 - 41

Sometimes when the lamp of faith burns low, when our sense of worth is at a low ebb, and we think that no-one cares, or that no-one could possibly love us, and we are without hope, then we experience love and forgiveness from those who have kind hearts and gentle faces, an open door and open hearts, and we know the overwhelming beauty of unconditional love, a love that we have hungered for since our birth, a hunger we have known as long as our hunger for air, and when it comes we can hardly believe it and we are surprised by joy.

George Herbert, an English poet of the 17th century, tells of an anguished night of the soul when he thought that his shriveled heart could never again support life, that never again would he be able to write verse, he would die like a flower in a late frost, but amazingly, he recovered, his life wasn't over, he was reprieved once again;

"And now in age I bud again,
After so many deaths I live and write;
I once more smell the dew and rain
And relish versing. O my only Light,
It cannot be
That I am he
On whom Thy tempests fell all night.
These are Thy wonders, Lord of love."

Yes, there is this amazing aspect of the grace of God, we are overwhelmed by it, we are surprised by joy.

Back in December '92 I was living the retirement I had planned. I was enjoying a full and happy life, when came a phone call from St. David's United Church in Calgary. I had the opportunity to serve God in new ways. I became Senior Minister to a large, vibrant church – in fact, the most active United Church in Canada.

I had the opportunity to preach to a large, responsive and appreciative congregation. I could share once again the glories of the gospel. I could use my pastoral skills. I could share my knowledge, my faith and my life. What a wonderful experience it was. God had overwhelmed me once again with his gift of grace: he surprised me with joy, and my cup runneth over.

This is the great theme and story of Christianity. Our God is a generous God:

a God who overwhelms us with his gifts,

a God full of surprises,

a God who pulls the rug from under us,

a God who turns the tables on us; and nowhere is there a greater surprise than that first Christmas when "The Lord of all Being, throned afar," appeared in the form of a little child. In the words of the old carol:

> "Who is he in yonder stall?
> At whose feet the shepherds fall?
> And the wonderful, unbelievable, glorious answer,
> 'Tis the Lord, the King of glory,
> Tis the Lord, O wondrous story,
> At his feet we humbly fall,
> Crown him, Crown him. Lord of all"

There is something wonderfully generous about our God who showers upon the unworthy the gift of his love. Who causes his blessed rain to fall on the just and the unjust alike.

This God of the unexpected who surprises us with joy…

This God who encounters the grief stricken on the road to Emmaus and gladdens their sad hearts…

This God who appears to the disillusioned disciples who had sorrowfully gone fishing and invites them to breakfast…

This God who comes to the refugee, far from home, lonely and lost in that desolate valley and assures him that he will be will be his companion wherever he may wander…

This God who comes to the hopeless like Saul Kane in Masefield's poem, "The Everlasting Mercy," who emerges from that English pub a new man, seeing the world a new place through new eyes...

"O glory of the lighted mind,
How dead I'd been, how dumb, how blind.
The station brook to my new eyes,
Was babbling out of paradise;
The waters rushing from the rain
Were singing Christ is risen again.
I thought all earthly creatures knelt
From rapture of the joy I felt,"

This God who comes to us when our lamp of self-worth burns low...
This God who comes to us through kind hearts and gentle faces and transforms us by his grace.

John Newton, born in 1725, was a slave trader. Early in life he lost his mother. At eleven he went to sea with his father. He was press-ganged into the navy. He deserted and was caught, flogged, and degraded. He wanted to kill himself. Eventually he became captain of a slave ship, then he had an awakening and took Holy Orders.

He rose from the depths of degradation, from being a self-designated wretch to a new man in Christ. Newton was to write a number of hymns during his 23 years as a rector but none charted his faith journey like the one that has, in recent years, had a rebirth in popularity:

"Amazing grace, how sweet the sound that saved a wretch like me!
I once was lost, but now am found, was blind but now I see.
'Twas grace that taught my heart to fear, and grace my heart relieved:
How precious did that grace appear the hour I first believed.
Thro' many dangers, toils, and snares, I have already come;
'Tis grace that brought me safe thus far, and grace will lead me home.
The Lord has promised good to me, this word my hope secures;
God will my shield and portion be as long as life endures..."

A Bundle on the Doorstep

"...and you will find the babe wrapped in swaddling clothes lying in a manger."

~Luke 2:12

My Associate minister at Minto United Church in Moose Jaw, Saskatchewan, for some years, was the Rev. Russell Young. Russell had just returned from Korea where for twelve years he had been a rural evangelist. His stories about conditions in Korea were always interesting and one in particular comes to mind at this time of the year.

On more than one occasion, he and his wife, Shirley, would hear a knock at their door but when they answered it, whoever had been there vanished into the night leaving behind on the doorstep a bundle of clothing containing, usually, a female child. For whatever reason, the mother of the child had decided that the child would have a better future with the strangers from abroad than with her own people.

It's a painful scene, this separation – forever - of a mother from her baby. We cannot imagine what heartbreak the mother experienced as she gazed into the face of her baby for the last time before abandoning her on a doorstep. She was taking a terrible chance, a risk that is difficult for us to understand, but in a land where a female child would not be as valued as a boy the little girl's future would be terribly precarious indeed. She could even be sold to be rid of her and to be of some value to her family.

Whatever the reason, there is a terrible portrayal of ugliness in this scene, almost as if we were reading in a city newspaper the story of a new-born child being found in a dumpster. But... the mother had chosen well. She had left her bundle on the doorstep of those who value all of God's children and whose meat it is to love one another as God loves us.

There is a part in the Christmas story that has always captivated me:

> *"...and you will find the baby wrapped in swaddling clothes lying in a manger."* ~ Luke 2:12

There is nothing more vulnerable than a baby; it is totally helpless, yet this is the medium by which our God chooses to enter the affairs of men and women in a new and dramatic revelation.

Our God, the creator and sustainer of this vast universe and everything in it; our God, whose Spirit permeates all he has made seeks kinship with his creation; our God who, in the beginning became one with the humans he created by breathing his Spirit into them and creating them for himself and for one another, chooses once again to establish his kinship with them and does so by becoming a little child and lying down on the doorstep of the world.

His original relationship has gone awry. He has established his relationship with the people by instructing them right and wrong and instilling in them the ability to choose, so that they might choose life and not death. He did so by driving them out of the garden when they disobeyed and by thundering forth from Mount Sinai when he established the ground rules of a covenant relationship whereby he would be their God and they would be his people.

In the years that followed the covenant was frequently dishonoured by the people but never by God. They learned that a covenant, unlike a contract, is still in effect until both parties give up and the nature of God is that he never gives up.

I saw this acted out one morning at the Sheep Gate in Jerusalem. Bedouin shepherds, in from the desert, met with townspeople who wanted to buy a lamb or kid for a special dinner. If the shepherd responded favourably to the man's request they would join hands and the bargaining would begin. It would end only when both decided to let go. The people often broke the covenant, when they entered the Promised Land. They turned to other gods and the fertility cults of the

Canaanites but God was ever true to them and still is today. He doesn't let go. He is always the waiting father.

The years that followed see a groping of the people to understand the true nature of the God they followed. We know from the Jacob saga that he is not like so many other gods: rooted to one spot, one hilltop or one shrine, but a God who travels, a God who assures the wanderer that he will always be with him no matter where he roams.

Isaiah tells us that He will be with us in the troubled times of life, the waters that would drown us and the fires that would consume us; He is the Lord our God and He loves us. And how does God love us? He loves us as a mother loves her baby and He holds us in the palm of his hand.

Still, some of the prophets told of a vengeful God, a cruel God and a God of retribution. And every year the Hebrews enacted the great deliverance of their forbearers from the land of Egypt, where He brought great plagues and slaughtered the first born children of the Egyptians and drowned the soldiers of Pharaoh. They believe of a God who cared for his children but a God greatly to be feared, and yet they awaited his coming and some sign from God that he had not deserted them.

Then one starry night a marvelous sight confronted a group of shepherds in the fields of Bethlehem, which sent them hastening to a stable where they found a little bundle of humanity - God's sign to them wrapped in swaddling clothes and lying in a manger. The significance of this is exemplified by the American poet, Walt Whitman, when he writes:

"He is not standing afar off waiting for us to draw nigh,
but a God who sought us out, striving ever to enter, trying doors, strategically planning,
making himself small as a child and lying down on the doorstep of the world.
The world, moved by the cry of a child, stealthily opened a door that had remained barred against the thundering tempest and avenging words,
took the child in and unwittingly let God through".

And so, through this bundle on the doorstep, God creates a new relationship with his people and reveals himself once and for all as a God of love who would never want us to fear.

Sometimes we hear the expression, "He dropped a bundle," to describe a gambler who has gambled and lost. Yet, here in the Christmas story it is God who drops a bundle, containing his only son, on the doorstep of the world. It appears like an awful gamble. It could have gone all wrong. He had chosen this peasant lass to be the mother of his child for he had to be fully human, with a human father and a human mother. And he had chosen the most common of people, this couple in the little hill village of Nazareth.

But when the baby was close to full term, a decree from the Emperor in Rome was read, by a Centurion in the village square, that all the world under the dominion of Rome had to be registered in a census and each person had to do it in his own town. This meant, for Joseph, Bethlehem, and so now the unborn son of God, is carried by his mother on a donkey on the long arduous journey through Samaria, past Jerusalem, to Bethlehem.

Arriving there, they find that the inn is full. The census has meant that there were many on the road and the innkeeper, perhaps like some of our modern hotels who advertise that there are no surprises, took a look at Mary and decided that here was a surprise that he and his guests could do without. He turned them away and missed the chance of a lifetime. Think of the sign he could have displayed above the door of his inn: "Jesus the Christ was born here."

If you visit the wee village of Ballater, Scotland, near Balmoral Castle, every store and sweetie shop displays the royal coat of arms above the door to tell the passerby that that they are purveyors to royalty. Or, if you go to Dumfries every pub or hotel lets all the world know that Rabbie Burns slept here. The Scots, of course, know a thing or two about making money, but this innkeeper missed the boat.

There's an enormous church built over the stable where Jesus was born. Hundreds of thousands of visitors visit the Church of the Nativity each year, but, the inn? Nobody knows where it is. There is, in Bethlehem, even to this day, a site visited by many expectant mothers. It is the Milk Grotto, a cave where tradition says this was the first stop the little family made to let Mary to feed the baby, Jesus, on their flight to Egypt. The legend goes on to say that some drops of her milk fell on the floor of the cave. Mothers ever since go there in large numbers to scrape the walls of the cave and then make a paste that they believe when eaten will assure a good supply of milk for their baby. Many go to the Milk Grotto which, of course, is marked by a church, but no-one looks for the inn. If Time Magazine were to list the biggest commercial opportunity missed in the last two millennia, surely the innkeeper in Bethlehem would top the list.

Yes, it was a gamble, God dropping this precious bundle of joy on the doorstep of the world. The child, while a hope for the poor, was a threat to the rich. While at one with the humble, it was at odds with the powerful. The promise of a new day for the oppressed was an upsetting factor for the status quo, and while it was a voice of hope for ordinary folks, it was a threat to the king on the throne.

Soon the streets resound with the tramp of soldiers' boots and the air is filled with the cries of mothers whose new born children are murdered. The little family has to flee through the desert wastes to Egypt. No gamble is without risk and this was a gamble that God was willing to make in order that the world would come to know how much he loved it:

> *"For God so loved the world that he gave his only son that those who believed in him would have everlasting life..."*-John 3:16

But, there was more to the coming of the child than that. God was also gambling on human kindness. God knew that the child would appeal to the finest part of our nature. God knew when he made us he made us in his image, he made us like him. He is love and when we live in love - the scriptures tell us - we live in him and he lives in us.

This is the basic nature of us. At the core we are beautiful, lovable and capable. Only our warped, mistaken beliefs about ourselves lead us to think that we are basically bad, that we are no good, that we are of little worth, that we are stupid or that we not acceptable.

Every time I work with people my solitary goal is to get them to have a radically new opinion of themselves. The goal of all counseling is to get people to see themselves as they really are and that is as a child of God, made in his image, with his nature. The truth is - and I base my life and career on this - we are all more lovable, more acceptable, nicer, more capable, and more lovable than we believe ourselves to be. To believe the worst about ourselves is the true sin from which Christ seeks to save us.

It wasn't as much of a gamble as it seemed to be, God lying down on the doorstep of the world and hoping that someone would take him in. For he knew that if humans acted as he had created them to do, they would take the baby in and he would find a home in the only place he could be at home - the only place on earth good enough, rich enough and large enough - in our hearts.

"Thou dids't leave Thy throne
And Thy kingly crown
When Thou camest to earth for me,
But in Bethlehem's Inn
There was found no room
For Thy holy nativity;
O come to my heart, Lord Jesus:
There is room in my heart for Thee.

When heaven's arches shall ring,
And her choirs shall sing
At Thy coming to victory,
Let Thy voice call me home,
Saying, "Yes there is room -
There is room at my side for thee!"
And my heart shall rejoice, Lord Jesus,
When Thou comest and callest for me."

~Emily Elliot

To Light a Penny Candle

"The real light which lightens every person was even then coming into the world"

~John 1:8

"The spirit of man is the candle of the Lord"

~Proverbs 20:27

Thomas Carlyle, that great man of letters, once said, "The older I grow , and I stand on the brink of eternity, the more comes back to me the first question in the Shorter Catechism,'What is the chief end of man?' and it's answer, 'The chief end of man is to glorify God and enjoy him for ever'." When I was ,thinking this week about my own childhood the words that came to me were;

> *Jesus bids us shine*
> *with a clear pure light,*
> *Like a little candle*
> *burning in the night.*
> *In this world is darkness;*
> *so let us shining,*
> *You in your small corner,*
> *and I in mine.*

Most of us will smile at the little girl who asked,"Mommy, please turn out the dark", but I am sure that there have been times in all our lives when we have wished that someone would 'turn out the dark'. And many times in the history of our Western civilisation people have made observations similar to that of Sir Edwar Grey in 1914, "

One by one the lights are going out".

It was a light that brought the Wise Men to Bethlehem; the light of a star. It brought them to the cradle of a little boy who grew up and said, *"I am the light of the world"* and turning to his followers he said, *"You are the light of the world".*

His coming was a light in a dark world but when his followers heard that they were to share his mandate - that they too were to be bearers of the light - they felt very inadequate. In the words of the old Irish ballad,

> *"They might as well have tried to catch a moonbeam, or light a penny candle from a star..."*
> ~Galway Bay, old Irish ballad

It was this star, this strange, new wonderful star, shining brightly in the dark sky of a decaying Roman Empire, which led the Wise Men and their camels over moor and mountain, field and fountain, to the little town of Bethlehem. So we at Christmas light candles as we commemorate the birth of Jesus.

Some modern candles are very beautiful. They are real works of art. Some are so beautiful that we are reluctant to light them. But they don't have to be works of art. Candles can be plain and ordinary and still be effective.

On my visits to Scotland I am tempted once again to go out to the garden shed and look once more for a long, lost tallow lamp worn by my father in the coal mine. It's a crude, primitive old thing... just a wick dipped in tallow which, when lit, would give off a yellow, sooty flame. That is probably why it is lost. Someone probably threw it away, but in the pitch black of the coal mine it gave enough light to work by.

Candles can be crude. They can be made of wax or tallow, nothing particularly beautiful. They don't need to be costly or delicate, coloured or ornate, nicely carved or perfumed. Even the core of the candle can be little more than a piece of string. In a dark room any unlit candle is invisible and of little worth until we put a match to it and the miracle of ignition takes place - an event that has fascinated human kind since the dawning of the ages.

As the cold candle is touched by a flame it begins to glow with a light and heat of its own. It becomes a golden spear on common wax. Now the invisible becomes visible, the worthless becomes useful and the common, ordinary wax or tallow taper becomes a thing of beauty, glowing with a golden flame.

Now, in a dark room we don't really see the candle. We see its flame and the things on which it casts its light. The candle is serving its purpose.

Once in the primordial darkness, at the beginning of time, God Said, "*Let there be light!*" and there was light. Things began to be, grow and live, all according to God's purpose in the light that he had made.

There was another time many years later, when the world was dark with a darkness of a different kind, and God said, "*Let there be light*" and there was light; the light which John says:

> "*The light which lightens every person was even then coming into the world*" ~John1:9

Here was the star to light the twisted string which is the heart of the common wax in every person. Here was the light which, by the miracle of divine ignition, brings forth the golden spear to lighten our way and the way of others.

To let our light shine is the nature of our calling. As Jesus said,

> "*When a lamp is lit it is not put under a meal tub but on a lamp stand where it gives light for everyone in the house. In the same way your light must shine before people so that they may see the good things that you do and praise your Father in heaven.*" ~Matthew 5:15-16

One Saturday night there was a car-train collision in Moosomin, Saskatchewan in which four teenagers were killed. One was our baby-sitter, Dianne, the daughter of our best friends on our first pastoral charge.

It was shattering news and as I drove to my first service at Fairlight, Saskatchewan, that awful Sunday morning I wondered what was I going to say to my two congregations in light of that awful disaster that had effected the lives of so many in those small communities. The words I kept recalling were: *"It is better to light a candle than to curse the darkness"*.

Later that day I found Rachel, Dianne's mother, writing a letter to the mother of the lad who had tried to race the train to the crossing and had killed himself and his three friends. As I saw Rachel write that letter I knew that a candle was being lit.

It is better to light a candle that to curse the darkness.

This is the choice that is ever before us. When life is unfair, when tragedy strikes or when the innocent suffer we can shake our fist at God. We can follow the advice of Job's wife to her suffering husband and *"curse God and die"*. We can curse the darkness that has befallen us, or... we can light a candle.

As we read in the Book of Proverbs:

> *"The spirit of the man is the candle of the Lord"*. -Proverbs 20:27

Over in England there is a magnificent village church built at a time when England was being ravaged by its worse civil war. In the porch are inscribed these words:

> *"In the year 1542, when things sacred were either demolished or profaned, this church was built by one whose singular praise it is to have done the best things in the worst of times and to have hoped them in the most calamitous"*.

A century and a half later Britain was again plunged into the darkness of fear as she stood alone and in constant fear of invasion. The news of the day was filled with the battles of Napoleon but in 1809, silently and without fanfare, five babies were born; Darwin, Lincoln, Chopin, Gladstone, Tennyson. Each in his own way would bring the light of knowledge, statesmanship, justice, beauty, truth and strength to bless the lives of humankind.

There is a memorial at Oxford, England which marks the place where two men, Bishops Latimer and Ridley, were burned at the stake for their beliefs. As the flames started, Latimer said,

> *"Cheer up Master Ridley, and play the man. By God's grace we shall this day light such a candle as shall never be put out".*

The spirit of man is the candle of the Lord.

Today, in our modern society, there is a great deal of darkness and we can at times feel overwhelmed by the magnitude of the problems that confront us. We can feel inadequate and powerless and may be tempted to curse the darkness but we know that we are not powerless for we are followers of Him who was the light of the world. As we embody the light of His love, our church becomes a redemptive force in our corner of their world.

Sometimes people who have just about given up on life come to our church seeking our help. Their world is a dark place and they are lost in it. They have lost faith in themselves and feel powerless to cope. It is then that we offer the candle of love, respect and caring; and, as they tentatively reach out and touch their almost lifeless candle to ours, the spark of life grows in them and soon their confidence shines. They see the way and they know that they are lovable, capable, and equal.

If we were to attempt to accomplish this by our own might and cleverness we would fail for we are all well aware of our inadequacies and weaknesses. But it is not ourselves who will do it. As Paul says, in the glorious fourth chapter of his second letter to the Church in Corinth:

> *"It is not ourselves we preach. We preach Jesus Christ as Lord, and ourselves as your servants for Jesus' sake. It is the God who said: 'Light will shine out of the darkness', who has made His light to shine in our hearts to illuminate them with the knowledge of the glory of God seen in the face of Jesus Christ".*
> ~2 Cor. 4:6-7

Paul goes on to say: *"Yet we who have this treasure are like common clay pots"*, reminding us that those who were God's spokespersons in the Old Testament, those who rallied to the call of the Master and those who became his disciples were common everyday folk. Many of them were seriously flawed, all of them sadly lacking at times and all of them far from perfect. Earthen vessels indeed, yet they were chosen to be repositories and dispensers of God's love.

Thus it was and thus it ever shall be.

God calls the imperfect, the ordinary, the common, to be his witnesses. We - all of us - have this treasure bestowed upon us by our God. We have it bestowed while we are still imperfect vessels, or (to change the metaphor) we who are common wax with plain, twisted string for a center, can become golden spears of light. We can become candles in the hand of God if we have the courage to hold our cold, lifeless, and common candles out to the light of Christ and see the miracle of divine ignition take place that our lives might be illumined by the light of his life.

We can see that our light will shine in the darkness of our world, "*You in your small corner, and I in mine*".

The spirit of man is the candle of the Lord. So come all ye faithful; come let us adore him, and let us light our penny candle from his star.

Love Will Find a Way

Drive down any back lane today
     and you will find discarded Christmas trees;
trees which only a short time ago,
     gaily decorated with tinsel and ornaments,
     stood ablaze with lights
       in a prominent place
       in our living rooms,
     have now been discarded
       and thrown out.
Some have been dumped
   ignominiously on garbage cans,
     while others are stuck
       upright in snow banks
         making a pathetic stab
         at past glory.
But each of them,
     their tinsel in shambles,
     their branches quite bare,
       are poor, sad semblances
         of the gaily decorated,
       brightly lit,
     sweet smelling works of nature,
       that was the focal point
     for so much of the festive season.

It is a sad ending indeed for such a beautiful decoration…
    but perhaps
      it symbolizes the way
        some of us feel about Christmas
          - a bit sad that it is all over.

Once when driving home I heard on the car radio a plaintive voice singing,
    "Why can't we keep Christmas for the rest of the year?"
      I heard it just that once
and it struck me as being the most melancholy Christmas song
I had ever heard.
      And yet, I suppose it is an authentic Christmas song
for it expresses a feeling many of us have had at one time or another.
Before Christmas
    we sat by the Christmas tree
      with its twinkling lights
        and shimmering decorations,
      and looked at the glistening tinsel;
        the beribboned wreath on the door…
The Christmas cards strung in colourful array
    and the flickering candles
      on the frosted Yule log…
    It is little wonder
that we would like
    to join with the singer
    and ask:
"Why can't we keep
  the colour and gaiety,
    the warmth and love,
    the peace and the joy
      of this blessed season
        for the rest of the year?'

Just a short time ago
    we went to church on Christmas eve
    and felt the magic of the holy night
      when the Saviour of the world was born.

The sanctuary was bathed in a rosy glow
   and the communion table
   was a flicker with candles,
      while out in the streets
         the multi-coloured lights
      of the gaily decorated houses
   would bring joy to the most reluctant heart.

Yes, we'd love to hold on
   to that warm, sentimental, magical feeling,
      and the spirit of goodwill that touches all
         for just a few days longer.

But it won't work.

We can stick the Christmas tree
   in the snow bank
   but the magic has gone.
We must rise from the manger
   and resume our daily tasks.
Now as the New Year beckons,
   we turn our backs on the manger
      and make decisions
   about how we will share with others,
      the gift we have been given.
That the message of Christmas
   may be heard and experienced
      in new and deeper ways in days to come.

Ahead lies the untrod path
   of a new year
      leading to new challenges.
   Before us is the book of our lives
      on whose blank pages will be recorded
         the diary of our days.
How can we
   who have heard the good news,

who have experienced new life,
    be obedient to God's call
       and be his witnesses?
There are two little words
    that I find to be essential
      when endeavouring to serve others.
I see them embedded in the Gospels.
    I see them prominent
      in the healing ministry of Jesus.
I see them in the tact of Paul
    as he - a stranger -
      writes to the saints in Rome.

These words are
    "respect" and "acceptance".

If we are to follow the great injunction -
    which undergirds all the joy of Christmas -
      "Love one another,"
    we must begin with respect and acceptance.
I firmly believe
    that affirmations of love
      and acts of giving,
        if not embedded in respect,
          are hollow affairs.
We cannot help whom we do not respect.
    and if we claim to be inclusive,
      but do not accept all God's children,
        our profession of love will be of no avail.
If I were asked to choose
    between being with someone who loved me
but did not respect me,
    and someone who respected me
      but did not love me,
    I would choose the latter.

Love without respect is a shabby affair.

I am convinced that
    if we do not respect people.
      we cannot help them.
    If we do not accept people,
      they will not trust us.
A hurting world awaits us
    as we step into a new year.

    God's great gift of unconditional love,
   offered without threat or coercion,
    in the form of a vulnerable child
      is needed by every person
        we will encounter in the days ahead.

We have been to the manger.

We have seen this thing that has happened,
    that the Lord has made known to us.
    We may have stashed the tree
      in the snow bank
        but, like Mary,
      we have kept all these things,
    pondering them in our hearts.
The joy of Christmas,
    the joy of knowing that God cares for us
      and through us and for all his children,
        is with us always...

    Even to the end of time.

Facing Up to Life

"Fight on my men!
I am wounded but I am not slain.
I'll lie me down and bleed awhile
and then I'll rise and fight again..."
~Sir Andrew Barton

"Do not be unhappy. All is for the best. We are playing a
good part in God's great scheme of things , arranged by God
himself and all is well..."
~ Edmund Wilson

This is the first Sunday in Lent. It is the season of the Church year, which can be seen as a valley, with the Transfiguration of Jesus at one end and the resurrection of our Lord at the other. In between is the descent into the valley of the shadow of death itself. In today's scripture we see Jesus setting out for Jerusalem. He begins his descent into the valley where he will encounter and confront every human terror and stare into the valley of the face of death itself.

After a successful ministry in the hill country of Galilee, where multitudes flocked to see him, where the crowds pressed in to hear him, where the sick and blind cried out for his healing touch, Jesus now sets his face toward Jerusalem where the High O Priests are plotting his arrest and where the Roman soldiers stand waiting with a cross.

This is a turning point in the ministry of Jesus.

In many ways it is the beginning of the end. Jesus is entering the last phase of his ministry. Mark catches the moment graphically. Jesus, now that he has set his face toward Jerusalem, fully aware of what lies ahead, is striding out manfully while his disciples who are filled with alarm are lagging behind.

Jesus, seeing their fear, takes them aside and speaks to them about the things that are going to happen to him. He tells them:

> "...Listen! We are going to Jerusalem where the Son of Man will be handed over to the Chief Priests and the teachers of the law. They will condemn him to death and turn him over to the Gentiles who will make fun of him, spit on him, whip him and kill him, but in three days he will rise to life..." ~ Matthew 18:19 – 20

The last line was lost on them. It was a prophetic statement of fact but I don't think the fears of the followers were allayed one bit. All they probably heard was the mocking, the whipping, and the killing. When the going got rough, and they thought their necks would be next their fears took over, they deserted him and Peter, we read, watched from afar.

Can you hear them as they followed him giving him words of encouragement? "Go on Jesus! We're right behind you; you can handle him. I'll hold your jacket."

What strikes me about Mark's passage, which is one of my favorites in Scripture, is the sheer courage of the man, Jesus.

There are many varieties of courage. There is the courage of the moment, when disaster happens and the adrenaline flows and we respond without considering the cost. We take the risk, we disregard our own safety and we take the necessary action to save a trapped person and many a person has become a hero on the spot of the moment.

Then there is the courage born of the belief that we are immune. It only happens to the other person.

When I worked in the coal mines I led a charmed life. I cheated death often. Indeed we made a game of it. When we carried maimed bodies out of the pit I never thought it could happen to me. I was immune.

Or perhaps we are fatalistic and our time is not yet. Like the old soldier saying to the new recruit: *"If your name isn't on the bullet it won't get you"*.

Over in Scotland where the most popular beer was McEwen's Pale Ale, a man was at a football match where people behind him were throwing bottles at the players. Some were falling short and were hitting the people around him giving them pretty sore heads. So he lifted up the tails of his coat and held them behind his head to make a buffer.

"Ach!" said the Scot beside him, *"if yer name's no on the bottle, it'll no hit ye"*.

"Aye", said the man, but ma' name's McEwen!"

Yes, there is the courage of the moment when we rise to the occasion, and there is the false courage of those who think they are immune. And there is the courage of the fatalist who thinks that his time is not yet. Then there is the courage of the person who, fully aware of the danger ahead, presses on and dares the devil to do his damnedest. This is the courage of Jesus who, knowing full well the terrible fate that lies ahead of him, presses on.

Courage, that loveliest of virtues.

Courage, how we admire it.

In wartime we reserve our highest decorations for those who express the ultimate expression of it in the service of others, without regard for personal safety.

Courage, how our hearts warm to it.

There comes to mind the words of Henley in his poem, *Invictus*:

"I am the master of my fate; I am the Captain of my soul..."

Do you know that when Henley wrote those words he was a patient in the old Royal Infirmary in Edinburgh? It was a dungeon of a place: dark, gloomy, cold and foreboding.

He writes a letter to his great friend, James Barrie:

"I was a patient in the old Infirmary in Edinburgh. I had heard vaguely about Lister and went there as a sort of forlorn hope on the chance of saving my foot, The great surgeon received me as he did a does everybody, with the greatest kindness, and

for twenty months I lay in one ward or another of that old place under his care. It was a desperate business but he saved my foot, and here I am."

And there he was folks! What was he doing in that old place during those twenty months of that desperate business but singing that he was the master of his fate, and the captain of his soul.

Now that is courage. The kind of courage we crave for the desperate times of our lives.

A courage like that exhibited by Sir Andrew Barton:

> *"Fight on my me!*
> *I am hurt but I am not slain;*
> *I'll lie me down and bleed awhile,*
> *And then I'll rise and fight again..."*

That's it!

We cannot expect life to be plain sailing. We know we will have our setbacks and disappointments. We know we can expect to be bowled over by the onslaught of life's storms and be left hors-de-combat by loss and illness. We cannot expect immunity. We will experience our share of tragedy and loss, but we pray for that resiliency that will enable us to come back and pick up the traces of life once again...

> *"I am hurt but I am not slain; I'll lie me down and bleed awhile, and then I'll rise and fight again."*

Courage, that lovely virtue without which we are less than human, for as Paul writes to Timothy:

> *"....the Spirit that God gives us is not the Spirit of fear, instead his Spirit fills us with power and love and self-control."*
> *q-2 Timothy 1:7*

Let me read you another letter, one written by the great explorer, Robert Falcon Scott, of the Antarctica, to his friend, J.S. Barrie. A letter found in the tent in the frozen wastes of Antarctica where Scott and his companions perished months before.

"We are pegging out in a very comfortless spot. Hoping this letter may be found and sent to you, I write a word of farewell. I want you to think well of me and my end. Goodbye, I am not afraid of the end but sad to miss many a simple pleasure I had planned for the future in our long marches. We are in a desperate state – feet frozen, etc. no fuel, and a long way from food, but it would do your heart good to be in our tent to hear our songs and our cheery conversations. We are very near the end. We did intend to finish ourselves when things proved like this but we have decided to die naturally without..."

I think it would do all our hearts good to stand outside that tent to hear the songs and cheery conversations of those stout-hearted men awaiting the inevitable.

It is not our basic make up to be timid.

The human baby is born with great courage but often the most well-meaning parents teach their children a multitude of fears; groundless, baseless, meaningless, silly fears which erode the endowed courage. The word for all parents is to never teach your children fear.

Some of us believe that by displaying anger, or shouting, or screaming, or making threatening facial expressions, or punishing, or by behaving in threatening ways we can make our children behave. Never taking into account that the fear we instill, or invite, will only diminish them and rob them of their courage and with it the very joy of living. Have you ever seen or known a person a timid person who enjoys life to the fullest?

A world renowned author said to me that it was her belief that all expressed anger is manipulative. The purpose of displaying anger is to induce fear into another so that they will conform their behaviour to fir our desires and wants.

Courage enhances us; fear diminishes us.

Without courage we may put up a good show but inside we know something is lacking.

Do you remember the story of the Wizard of Oz? Dorothy and her companions the Scarecrow, the Tim Woodman and Toto, her little dog, were following the Yellow Brick Road through the thick woods when there came a great roar and a great lion bounded out of the trees onto the path. With one blow of his paw he sent the Scarecrow flying, his stuffing scattered. With another blow he knocked over the Tin Woodsman. Toto ran barking toward the Lion and Dorothy, fearing Toto would be killed, slapped the Lion on the nose as hard as she could and called him am coward for trying to bite a little dog.

"I know it", said the Lion, hanging his head with shame. "I've always been a coward but how can I help it"?

"What make you a coward?" asked Dorothy.

"I suppose I've always been that way', sod the Lion, "but I have learned that if I roared very loudly every living thing was frightened and got out of my way, but if any other animal had ever tried to fight me I should have run away, I'm, such a coward".

When he learned that Dorothy and her friends were on their way to see the Wizard, the Scarecrow to get brains, the Woodsman to get a heart, and Dorothy to be sent back to Kansas, the Lion decided to join them to get the Wizard to give him courage.

"For," said the Lion, "my life is simply unbearable without a bit of courage."

Indeed life is unbearable for all of us when we lose our courage and fear paralyzes us.

Jesus knew how fear and lack of courage could rob people of the joy of living. He came to show us a better way knowing that God had not given us the spirit of fear. Wherever fear comes from it, does not come from God. Others may teach fear, God does not.

All around us, in our communities and in our church, there are fearful people looking for ways to cope with their fears. We all need friends to support us when our courage deserts us and fear takes over. No matter what the situation that is taking away the person's quality of life, I know that the root cause will be fear, however if manifests itself.

If courage is the loveliest of virtues surely fear is the most demeaning. Most of our fears are groundless. They are the unresolved issues of childhood, vestiges of past terrors experienced when we were small, helpless and inadequate against the threats, angers, manipulations and neglect of those who exercised their control and power over us. Of those who criticized, ridiculed, ignored, threatened and embarrassed us when we were small and lived in the valley of the giants.

All of us carry wounds from our childhood into the present and when a situation or a confrontation arises, which contains similarities to that era, we are virtually called into the boss's office, the policeman waves us over, our spouse walks out on us, we think we are going to fall, we drop a costly piece of china or we forgot the important meeting. We 'rubber band' our present situation to that early scene. We bring the past to the present and our fear makes us vulnerable, weak, inadequate, ashamed, stupid, or anxious. Fear: the most debilitating, debasing and worthless of emotions.

When I do counseling I know that regardless of the presenting problem, the underlying issue will be fear. My goal in counseling is to replace fear and helplessness with courage and hope through the power of love.

Jesus encountered many fearful people in his travels:
a disciple afraid to step out of the boat,
a woman afraid to admit that she touched him,
a young man afraid to give up his riches,
a priest afraid to cross the road to help an injured man,
a king afraid that the new born child would dethrone him,
an official afraid to be seen with him in daylight, a high priest afraid of losing his authority,
a man afraid to make it into the water, Pilot afraid to do his duty,
a Disciple afraid to be identified as his follower, and;
a group of followers lagging behind now that He is on a collision course with the authorities.

Like children, they - like us in our fears - prayed that the world would change, but Jesus didn't change the world. He offered them the power to change themselves and no longer be afraid, knowing that His love would cast out their fears.

When Winston Churchill's daughter said that his greatest gift to the British people was he gave them courage, he replied, "No, I helped them to find their own courage."

Jesus offered his followers courage: the ability to face life as he did with his face steadfast toward the future. One didn't accept. They called him the Rich Young Ruler and artists down through the ages have caught the slump of his shoulders as he turned sorrowfully away. To those who did accept his offer he gave the power to become children of God and members of his kingdom.

That offer is as available now, to each and every one of us, as it was then. The task of the Church today is to be the nurturing community through which the courage of Jesus becomes incarnate in the lives of frightened people.

"Fear not" is the first message from the Heralds of his coming and it is repeated like a drumbeat over and over throughout the pages of the New Testament. If we ask, "Why did Jesus come?" and posit the answer, "He came to do away with fear". Then read one of the Gospels and we will end up agreeing, "Yes, He came to banish fear. He came to rid humanity from fear and replace it with courage and hope. Any church that preaches fear and practices power is not worth its salt.

The disciples, we read, followed him from afar. But that isn't the whole story. These men and women did find the courage to follow Him. But they only found that courage when they shared His Faith, when they practiced His acts of mercy and loving kindness, and when they - like Him - could put their lives completely into God's hands and trust Him while they served Him, aware that nothing could separate them from the love of God in Christ Jesus his Son.

Perhaps the clue to this courage is in another letter found in that same tent near the South Pole where Scott and his stouthearted companions died. A letter from Edmund Wilson to his wife, found on his frozen body:

> "Do not be unhappy; all is for the best. We are playing a good part in God's great scheme of things arranged by God himself and all is well."

Surely this is the foundation of all courage: to be assured that we are plating a good part in God's great scheme of things and all is well.

I Have No Regrets

"Peter began to curse and he swore an oath, I do not know the man."

~ Matthew 26:74

"I have no regrets."

These were the words of Bridget Bardot when she was interviewed after reaching a birthday which definitely made her middle aged. Now, it may be somewhat difficult to conjure up images of the French sex kitten as middle-aged, but it is even more difficult to imagine that she can reflect on the way that she has come to this point - the tempestuous life that she has led - and still be able to say: "I have no regrets."

The memory that came to me as I reflected on these words was of standing on the balcony of the church of the Gallicantu, or Church of the Cock Crow, in Jerusalem. This is a modern church made of the beautiful Jerusalem limestone but tradition has it that this modern church is built on the sight of the place where Jesus was taken and held after being arrested that night in the garden.

Certainly there is evidence that there have been churches on this site for countless years. We can identify their features going back to the remains of the Crusader's church atop the Byzantine church and then back to the primitive Christian church.

In the basement there are the cells hollowed out of the rock. More important below us is a recent excavation which has revealed a courtyard right where the Bible said it would be and beside it a flight of stairs is now being excavated.

A shiver goes through me; this place has a ring of authenticity. Those are the steps that Jesus ascended; this is the courtyard where people warmed themselves by the fire; this is the place where Peter heard the Clarian of the dawn.

In an uncanny way when, while Bob and Ethel Dunn and I were standing on the balcony taking pictures of the ancient city of David, now outside the city walls (the rest of my tour group having moved on) somewhere down there among the rooftops of the ancient city we too heard a cock crow and I remembered Peter.

Peter, the big fisherman, certainly couldn't say, "I have no regrets" that night in the court yard as he stood warming himself by the fire. Only a short time before he and the rest of the disciples had shared a Passover meal with Jesus and had gone out singing to the Mount of Olives.

It was there that Jesus said to them, "all of you will run away and leave me".

That was the second bomb shell of the evening, earlier Jesus had said," one of you will betray me", and now this, "all of you will run away and leave me".

It was more than Peter could stand, and I can just see the big fisherman drawing himself up to his full height and declaring vehemently, "I will never leave you even if all the rest do. I am ready to go to prison, even to die for you Lord."

But Jesus seeing the frailty of the man said sorrowfully, "I tell you Peter before the cock crows twice you will deny me thrice."

And then it happened just as Jesus said it would. After the initial show of resistance in the garden of Gethsemane among the olive trees the disciples, including Peter, ran away to save their own skins.

The soldiers took Jesus to the house of the High Priest and Peter anxiously wanting to know what happened to him but not at all keen to be associated with him followed, the Bible tells us, from afar. Then Peter stood with the guards and the servants by the fire to await the outcome.

It was then that it happened, a servant lass from the house of the High Priest saw Peter there by the fire and looking straight at him said, "You also were with Jesus, the Galilean".

But Peter denied it saying, "I do not know what you are talking about," and he edged away from the fire into the shadows by the gateway where he wouldn't be so conspicuous. But the woman wasn't satisfied. She wouldn't let go and Peter was horrified to see that she was moving in amongst the crowd of bystanders, blabbing to them and saying this man is one of them.

Again Peter denies it and hopes that is the end of it. He certainly doesn't want people to know. The cold night drags slowly by and the crowd in the court yard would no doubt speculate about the man who was arrested and who his followers were.

Then yet another person pointed the finger at Peter and said "Certainly you are one of them, for you are a Galilean. I can tell by your accent".

At this third accusation Peter reacted even more strongly, he cursed and swore in his rough fisherman's tongue that he did not even know the man, and immediately the cock crowed twice and, horror of horrors, it was just then that Peter saw Jesus, who was being led through the court yard, turn and look at him. Peter remembered how Jesus had said, "Before the cock crows twice you will deny me thrice". Peter turned his back on the circle of light in the courtyard and went out in the darkness and wept.

I have no regrets.

What a wonderful thing to be able to say. Unfortunately through the misuse of memory and the lack of faith we can ruin our lives and rob ourselves of the joy of living through our vain regrets. Usually we do this by casting our thoughts backwards down the road we have travelled saying if only, if only, if only. If only I had used my head, if only my father hadn't been a drinker, if only I hadn't given them the car that night, if only I hadn't listened to them, if only my mother had understood me... if only, if only, if only.

This is the stuff of vain regret, and it's available to all of us. To revisit the past to focus on our misdeeds and our misfortunes is a sure way to depression and hopelessness, which robs us of our past, cheats us of our present, and steals our future.

The present and our future belong to those who use God's great gift of memory to enhance their life, for memory like all of Gods gifts can be used and misused. It can be a blessing or a curse; we can use it selectively to review our lives or present it as a vale of tears.

I'm sure you have met people like that whose lives when they tell you about it is one long litany of misfortune and justices and wrong doing. Having relived that painful past they become truly depressed, lethargic and woebegone. Or, we can use the great gift of memory God has given us to enhance our life.

As J.M. Barrie, the Scottish playwright once aptly put it:
"*God gave us memory that we might have roses in December*".

Let me read you the words of Judge Moloch of Ontario on his 86th birthday:

> "*I am still at work with my hand to the plow and my face to the future, the shadows of evening lengthen about me but morning is in my heart, I have had various fields of labour and full contact with men and things and I have warmed both hands at the fire of life. The testimony I bear is this, that the castle of enchantment is not behind me it is still before me, and daily I catch glimpses of its battlements and towers , the rich spoils of memory are mine, mine too are the precious things of today, books flowers, pictures, nature and sport. The first day of May is still an enchanted day for me, the best thing of all is friendship, the best of life is always farther on, and its real lure is hidden from our eyes somewhere beyond the hills of time.*"

What a beautiful statement from an eighty six year old man, from a man who has evening gathering about him but with morning in his heart. There is nothing here to suggest that he led a perfect life, nothing to suggest that he never made a mistake. He warmed both hands at the fire of life and he said the rich spoils of memory are mine.

When the Knights of the Round Table set out to look for the Holy Grail, they knew that only the pure in heart hoped to see it. And so Sir Percival, recalling his own past, began to fear that his seeking was hopeless:

"Then every evil word I had ever spoken, and every evil thought I have ever thought of, and every evil deed I have ever did awoke and cried this quest is not for thee, none but the pure at heart then every evil memory that comes from our past condemns us, and we cannot look on the face of God, that is if we live under the law on the other side of Easter."

But as the author of the fourth gospel reminds us, the law was given through Moses, grace and truth came through Jesus Christ. And from his fullness we have all received grace heaped apron grace. That is what Jesus offers, his grace to atone for our past.

It is yours to cleanse the heart, to sanctify the soul, to pour fresh life on every part and you create the whole. Regret is, as I am sure you are aware, rampant in our society. As you listen to this sermon, you may be getting in touch with some of your own vain regrets. Regret has been around for a long time. The children of Israel experienced it when they were escaping slavery in Egypt, no sooner have they achieved their freedom, then they began to regret it, and grumbled that they would have been better off if they had stayed as slaves rather than starve to death out here in the desert. If only we hadn't listened to Moses... If only we had appreciative of what we had... If only, if only, if only...

The story of the Exodus is a tale of contrast. It tells of the regrets of the people of Israel and the faith of Moses; their lack of trust in Gods ability to provide for their survival and the complete faith of Moses who endured. The book of Hebrews tells us *"as seeing him who is invisible"*. The lack of faith of Israel is a real motif in the Exodus narrative and, by a series of acted parables, Israel is taught that the first requirement of the people of God is to trust God come what may. The water that came from the rock, the flock of quails, the finding of the manna... All are part of the teaching that the hallmark of fitness to do Gods bidding is to rely on his providence day by day.

Do you think that's what Peter's problem was that night by the fire? Was it his lack of faith in the providence of God that made him denies his Lord and filled him with vain regret? Yes, Peter followed Jesus afar off. He was afraid to be too closely identified with him lest he too ended up on a cross and would regret he ever met the man.

"I tell you I am not one of them I do not know the man...".

Oh Peter, Peter, Peter! I wonder how often those words came back to haunt you. But, that wasn't the whole story of Peter. The road didn't end that night in the court yard. Peter went out in the night and wept, yes, but Peter, the big fisherman with the coarse tongue, the rough man with a Galilean accent, filled with regret, found his faith With the grace of God, he was able to forgive himself for his cowardice and betrayal and was then able to fulfill the potential that Jesus had seen in him the day he called him the Rock.

Yes, Peter found his faith and in finding his faith was able to let go of his vain regrets and found himself. He discovered the in events following that night the cock crow that God was as good as his word and, with that faith, he set out over the Roman roads to proclaim the good news that we don't have to live with our vain regrets. Jesus has forgiven us.

Church tradition has it that Peter too had to eventually to face his cross, and he asked to be crucified upside down. I have no regrets.

With Paul he faced his executioner and he could say:

> "*I am ready on the point of being sacrificed; the time of my departure has come. I have fought the good fight, I have finished the race, I have kept the faith, henceforth is laid up for me the crown of righteousness, which the Lord, the righteous judge will award to me on that day, and not only to me, but also to all who loved his appearing.*" 2 Timothy 4:7,8

I have no regrets.

First Pick at the Garbage

"What's treasure to one may be trash to another"
~American Proverb

"God see the little sparrow fall"
~Matthew 10:29

Over one hundred years ago Robert Louis Stevenson wrote:

"... The world is so full of a number of things I am sure we should all be as happy as kings..."

I wonder what he would say today if he were to follow us around a shopping centre and see the number of things that we carry home and stockpile in our basements, cupboards, and freezers.

Do you know that those who settled these vast prairies considered nineteen items to be essential in order to survive? But, if you ask the folks of today what they would need, they would list several hundred items. Furthermore, all of these things are readily available to most of us. We are an affluent society and even the ordinary family accumulates far more than they need.

Thirty years ago, Russell Baker wrote in the N.Y Times (Feb.22, 1968): "We live in an environment whose principle product is garbage." We have memories of a barge full of garbage being turned away from country after country and we have coined the phrase: "Not in my back yard".

Our houses regularly get filled with so much junk that getting rid of it has become a major problem. Magazines and newspapers, some of which haven't even been read, pile up. Boxes, bottles, wrapping paper, clothes, knickknacks, toys, plastic pails and containers of every shape and size pile up unless we ruthlessly throw them out or take them to the recycling depot.

I don't know whether it's because I'm a Scotsman or not, but I am continually flabbergasted at some of the things I find my wife has thrown in the garbage. When we lived in Saskatchewan we had a burning barrel and I was forever taking stuff back into the house saying to Joy: "Look what I found in the garbage, I almost burned it!" And she would shake her head and point out that it was cracked or chipped, or there was a piece missing and I would have to reluctantly return and commit perfectly good stuff to the flames. I dread my wife saying that we need to clean out the garage or the basement for I know she wants to get rid of some of my things. Usually she waits until I have gone somewhere for a couple of days then she gets busy and throws my stuff out, or donate it to a friend's garage sale, and hopes that I won't miss it.

My friends can still get me upset by mentioning my perfectly good gas barbecue that I had on standby after my kids bought me a new one. Now I know that it had been standing around for a number of years but not only did she get rid of it, she paid a man to haul it away! A perfectly good barbeque! I'm sure he couldn't believe his luck.

Nowadays we accumulate so much stuff we have to decide what to keep and what to get rid of. When a family moves there are usually some healthy arguments about what stays and what goes. My mother used to say:

"Keep a thing for seven years and you will find a use for it."

And I am my mother's son. On the other hand, my wife sees no value in all that old stuff.

No one, as far as I know, has made a study of couples in this regard but I think they come in pairs, usually there is a keeper married to a chucker and it is a recipe for conflict. I'm sure that one of the biggest dreads of folks who move into seniors Citizen Lodge is that they have to dispose of a lifetime of accumulated treasures.

Now, any immigrant to this country knows that you could live well on what Canadians throw away. When I worked as an installer for the

Bell Telephone Company in Montreal, I would encounter immigrant families living in the basement of small apartment buildings where they would live rent free for providing janitorial services. Of course, part of the bounty was that they would get first pick at the garbage. Eventually, by dint of hard work, frugal living and shared accommodation - several families in one apartment - they would save enough money to buy the building. They became the landlords but the always inserted a clause in the lease, "I still get first pick at the garbage".

Some time ago Bev Longstaff, a city councilor in Calgary, was advocating that the city's landfill be opened up to the public. Well, I can hardly wait. That's a veritable gold mine out there! I have heard from folks in our congregation, who winter south, that down in Arizona they have wonderful dump parties. What a fine way to spend an afternoon. I have had many a profitable afternoon in the nuisance grounds in Saskatchewan, much to my wife's chagrin.

Of course, today we have a variety of things designed to be thrown away. They are disposable. We have paper plates, cups, napkins, and what mother of young children does not appreciate disposable diapers? We also have a whole array of devices, lighters, cameras, razors, etcetera… all designed to be used and thrown away, disposable, just like the millions of dollars worth of space junk abandoned in space because it costs less to leave it than to retrieve it.

Disposable is a word used for those things we want to use then get rid of. Sometimes on television or in films we see men and women being regarded as disposable:

"Waste them!", "Blow him away!" or "Get rid of them."

Now, there have always been times when people have been regarded as disposable. The pyramids were built to last forever, but the slaves who labored to build them were as disposable as the scaffolding they worked on.

In the coal mine in which I worked in Scotland, men were considered disposable. It was commonly believed that to make a mine safe would price coal out of the market, so a blind eye was turned to high levels of gas and obvious safety hazards. Death and injuries were frequent visitors to coalmining homes. Miners and their limbs were disposable. Likewise, when the fish wife came around the doors selling her "silver darlings" she would sing:

*"...Buy my caller herring' they're bonnie fish and wholesome eating, Buy my caller herring new drawn frae the Forth..." ~*Caller Herrin'

But she adds the reminder:

"...You ca' them caller herring, I ca' them lives o' men..."

She knew that fishermen, who put out into the North Sea, sometimes paid for the fish with their lives. Thus she had a kinship with the miners of our village. They were indeed disposable.

It is a terrible thought that any human being should be considered disposable, and yet many in our modern society do not think that they themselves are of much value. Sometimes we will hear someone ask, or state: "Does my life really matter?" or "I don't see any point of living any more..." or "Why doesn't God take me?" or "I'm no use to anyone, and anyway, nobody cares..." or even, "I'm just in the way..."

Nobody wants them. Somehow the false and terrible message has got through to them. "I'm of no use..." or "You'd be better off without me..." And what are we to say? Or perhaps there has been a tragedy: a drunk driver kills a beautiful teenager, a mother dies a slow painful death, a good man suffers terribly, hundreds die in an earthquake, a ferry boat capsizes and hundreds are drowned, or a child is lost through the ice.

The question inevitable is: Does God care? Does God consider people disposable? Does God care?

This is no new question. It came up in the course of Jesus' ministry, and the answer we find the Master giving is that in God's sight no one is without worth. A sparrow falls to the ground. In our view sparrows are ten a penny, But Jesus says:

"Not a sparrow falls to the ground without your Father knowing about it. So don't be afraid, God sees the little sparrow

fall and you are much more valuable than a whole flock of sparrows". ~ Matthew 10:29

Every man and woman is precious in the eyes of God. And as Jesus encounters those whom the society of his time were apt to consider worthless he treated them all with respect .He saw everyone he encountered as his brothers and sisters, as children of the same father and of infinite worth. When we examine the life of Jesus the notion of human disposability must be banished from our minds and hearts.

Think of what was done to him. As Peter said to the leaders of the Temple:

*"You handed him over to the authorities, and you rejected him in Pilot's presence. He was holy and good but you rejected him and asked for the freedom of Barabbas instead" ~*Acts 3:14

When Jesus went to the cross there is no doubt that he was considered to be disposable for the cross was the way to get rid of the misfits and undesirables. For us, the crucifixion was a terrible event but for the Romans it was a matter of small importance. During the Maccabean revolt they crucified the rebels by the thousands and the highways of Palestine were lined with dying men on crosses and their cries filled the air. So when Jesus went to the cross he joined the long procession of those who were nuisances and undesirable and descended into the hell of the despised and rejected.

The Christ whom we worship was regarded a fodder for the scrap heap and has been through the agony of feeling deserted by God and man. The cross was at Golgotha the place of the skull, the city garbage dump. Jesus was treated like so much garbage. But as Peter said to the High Priest, "The stone you rejected turned out to be the most important. You killed him." But a funny thing happened on the way to the dump. God raised him from the dead - and took him home. God had first pick at the garbage.

Jesus says to our troubled world, where many are insecure and unsure of their worth, they treated me as disposable and they found out that I wasn't. Neither are you! You are a child of God. A person of real worth. You, just as you are, are God's gift to the world. When God made you he knew what he was doing. For, as one teenager put it, "God don't make no junk!"

So, always remember: when you are down in the dumps, God has first pick at the garbage.

The Elephant in the Living Room

"Hosanna, Loud Hosanna the happy children sang,
Through pillared court and temple the joyful anthem rang."
~Jenette Threefall

A young boy came home from school one day to find an enormous elephant standing right in the middle of the living room and, as if that wasn't bad enough, everyone in the house was ignoring it and pretending that it wasn't there.

There sat his father reading his paper as usual; his mother was fussing around in the kitchen and other members of the family came and went, but no one mentioned the elephant.

Not only was the elephant not mentioned by family members, it wasn't discussed outside the home either. You would think that good friends would have mentioned the elephant for surely some of them were aware of its presence but because the family never spoke about it, the friends didn't bring it up either.

Sometimes when mutual friends met they would gossip a bit about the beast but they felt powerless to intervene. There was one very concerned friend who felt that it was somehow his responsibility to bring the matter into the open. After all it isn't easy to carry on a meaningful conversation when there is an elephant between you. But... every time he cleared his throat to make a determined effort to broach the matter one of the family would change the subject, or suggest that he have another drink, or ask him if he would like to stay for supper and the time never seemed quite right to talk about the elephant.

The neighbours suspected something amiss in the home for, as you can imagine, an elephant isn't the easiest thing to keep to yourself. But no matter how many hints they dropped, the pretense went on and soon they to learned to go along with it.

Even at church, when the minister preached at great length about the dangers of elephants around the home, none of the family thought that it might be their elephant he was talking about. When the Lenten study group discussed other lands - where the elephants were so numerous that they sometimes destroyed whole villages - and what great work the Church was doing among the elephant-plagued people of that land, the lady of the house didn't feel free to mention the elephant in her home for the rest of the group would wonder how this could be, seeing she attended Church so regularly, was a faithful worker in the United Church Women and wasn't her husband an Elder on the session? So she kept the elephant to herself.

One day a man with a large suitcase came around the doors selling a variety of products designed to help harried housewives. Among the patent medicines she saw a bottle of large pills guaranteed to eliminate elephants and other large objects before your eyes. At last she had the solution. Alas, although she took them faithfully after every meal, they succeeded only in making her drowsy and while the elephant did indeed disappear every time she let her heavy eyelids close, there he was as large as life when the drowsiness wore off and she opened her eyes again.

Her husband, without saying much about it, tried to get rid of the elephant by using a type of vanishing cream he got in a plain brown wrapper from a mail order house. He'd seen the advertisement in a Men's magazine which guaranteed remarkable results: if the elephant didn't disappear overnight, it surely would in a short time. A money back guarantee if there wasn't a significant change in the size of the elephant. The pictures of shrunken elephants which accompanied the ad were convincing testimony indeed. But it didn't work. Oh there were times when he was quite convinced that the elephant was getting smaller - not nearly as big as before - but deep down he knew that he was kidding himself. So, he reverted to the old game of pretending that the elephant wasn't there.

It was around this time that his wife decided to see their family doctor. She wasn't feeling up to par, she told him. She wasn't sleeping as well as she used to and was frequently depressed. She told him about her headaches, her backaches and her stomachaches for these are all the ailments of the respectable. She didn't tell him about the elephant. She was too ashamed to, and, after all, she reasoned, what could the doctor do about an elephant? The medicine he prescribes helped her quite a bit, she thought, but it didn't have any effect on the elephant.

One day things got so bad that the couple decided to see their minister to talk over a few problems, they said, and this they did for a while until their minister said:

"It sounds as if you have an elephant in your home."

Well, that was a bit of a shocker, but what a relief to be able to talk to someone about it. After they had spent some time talking openly about their elephant, their minister suggested that they join a group that met regularly at the church. Everyone in the group, he told them, had one thing in common; they all had an elephant in their living room.

It almost floored them to realize that there were so many elephants in the community, especially up here on the North Hill. They thought they were mostly down on River Street or the East End, and they weren't too sure they wanted to get involved with a crowd like that, but their minister, seeing their hesitation, said,

"How would you like to have a couple from the church call on you and go with you to the first meeting?"

Their first surprise came when they answered their door bell on the night of the meeting. There on the doorstep was a teacher from one of the high schools and his wife, a nurse up at the hospital. They saw them in church every Sunday and who would have thought that they had any problems at all, but they assured them that they had an elephant too. The next surprise was at the group where they were greeted warmly by the members each one of whom wore a large badge the shape of an elephant. They introduced themselves by saying,

"Hi, I'm Jim, or Joan, or Larry, or Margaret and I have an elephant problem too..."

Suddenly they felt a sense of belonging such as they hadn't experienced for years. The next step, they were told, was to ask God to help them do something about the elephant for they realized that without him they were powerless. It wasn't easy, after all, for no one likes to admit that he is a failure, but the presence of the elephant had driven them to the brink of despair and if this was the way back to normal living, they were willing to give it a try.

Most people, at one time or another, have an elephant in their living room. For some it is a terrifying experience, for others it is a source of shame and disgrace. For others it is a passing phase but its searing memory lingers on. For yet others, their elephant has been around so long that they accept its terrible presence and destructive effect on their family life with futile and hopeless resignation.

The elephant may be a handicapped child in the backroom or out of sight in an institution. It may be the breakup of a daughter's marriage or a son living common-law. Perhaps you have an alcoholic spouse or a pregnant teenage daughter or a gay son. Could it be that one of your family is mentally ill and receiving psychiatric help, or are your parents heading for divorce? Perhaps you discover that your son is selling dope or your husband has strayed from the fold. Could it be that your uncle is a child molester or your brother is a thief?

The elephants in our living rooms. They just don't happen to decent church going people like us. We don't dare admit such a possibility to our fellow Christians, or even to ourselves and our own family, so we pretend that everything is all right with us and we live with our fears and keep our disgrace to ourselves.

That wasn't the way it was with Jesus. When he saw two men in the temple, one wearing the robes of piety, praying, "I thank God that I am better than others", and the other, wearing an Elephant badge, praying, "God have pity on me for I am a failure." He said,

> "This man, and not the other, was right with God when he went home…" ~Luke 18:14

And, nowhere is the badge that Jesus wore more evident than on his triumphal entry into Jerusalem and during the events that were to follow. Throughout his ministry he so identified with the moral and social rejects of his day that he was put to death as one of them.

On that Palm Sunday, when the crowds lined the roadway to sing hosannas to the king, the badge he wore so blatantly was that of the lowly, the despised, the misfit and the failure. During the days that followed the badge he wore got him into more and more trouble until in the end he was persecuted to death.

Thus Jesus joined the long procession of society's failures, misfits, and unworthies and descended into the hell of rejection.

But that isn't the end, is it? For this Jesus, this man with the stigma; this misfit rejected by the builders, became the cornerstone of the new community. This misfit became the source of new life and hope for all who dared wear his badge. This misfit - this man with the elephant badge - was raised from his hell to mark the dawning of a new day.

This mysterious process repeats itself in today's society where the stigma (if we are willing to risk it) becomes the badge of entry and acceptance into the fellowship of those who wear the same stigma.

And through this redeeming fellowship we learn to accept and be accepted, and to love and be loved.

I Meet the Elephant

I first met the Elephant when browsing through books in the study of my good friend the Rev. Dr. Bruce McIntyre. In "Love Marriage and Trading Stamps" by Richard Reesor, I saw a drawing of an elephant in a house.

Sometime later when writing a sermon for Palm Sunday the theme of the Elephant came to mind and the words simply flowed onto the paper. It was the easiest and quickest sermon I ever wrote. So much so that I wondered how much came out of Reesor's book. When I checked I found that it contained only the original idea. I broadcast the Elephant over CHAB from Minto United Church, Moose Jaw, on Palm Sunday 1973.

The Elephant became popular. When Minto Family Life Education Centre had a book table at a meeting of Saskatchewan Conference of the United Church of Canada in Saskatoon copies of the Elephant was given out as freebies and many ministers went home with a copy. The Lutheran Church asked permission to print five thousand copies for distribution throughout their churches.

When I moved to McKillop United Church in Lethbridge I preached the Elephant on the first Palm Sunday. A Sunday School teacher asked if I had to change it much. I told her that to make it relevant to Lethbridge I changed Moose Jaw's notorious River Street to Second Ave. and the South Hill became North Side. But that wasn't what she meant. She had seen the Elephant in the Living Room story in an AADAC publication. She brought me a copy and sure enough there was my Elephant sermon with all the religious parts and my name edited out. Next Sunday I told the congregation my Elephant had beaten me to Lethbridge, but, I added, it was a very truncated version.

One Saturday I answered my phone and it was a Chaplain friend of mine calling from Nova Scotia. He had been asked to preach in a large church and told the Secretary that his sermon would be: "The Elephant in the Living Room". Into the local newspaper and the Church bulletin it went then on Saturday he discovered he had mislaid his copy hence the phone call, He taped my wife, Joy, reading it over the phone then spent hours transcribing it.

A number of times people have told me that their minister read 'The Elephant' during worship. This pleases me greatly.

Enjoy my Elephant.

He Lives in Me

"There is a green hill far away, outside a city wall..."
~Cecil Francis Alexander

Tucked away in the maple-clad mountains of Argenteuil County in Quebec there is a lonely hill crowned by a scene which, when I first saw it, filled me with awe.

I had followed a winding path that encircled the hill as it sought the summit and when I reached the top there, facing me, was the scene of the crucifixion: a massive tableau of larger than life bronze figures with the cross of Jesus towering over all.

The statues, I learned, were created and cast in Belgium. They were shipped to Canada for safe keeping when war was threatening and now they crown that lonely hill. There was Jesus, flanked by the two thieves while below were the Roman soldiers, the disciples, and huddled together, the grieving women. It was magnificent.

There had been an attempt to create in the embankment, at the side of the clearing, an empty tomb but it was easily missed. The real focal point was this magnificent portrayal of the Crucifixion on Good Friday.

Easter falls far short of Good Friday when it comes to art. After all, how do you depict the resurrection in paint or charcoal, bronze or marble? Picasso produced forty paintings of the Crucifixion. Not one of the Resurrection.

The events leading up to Easter, like that other great Christian festival, Christmas, lend themselves well to art. The events of Holy Week, like the Christmas story, have everything that makes for great theatre. It is a time of high drama with a great cast of villains, traitors, persecutors and victims...

It has treachery and tragedy...
It has high adventure and apathy...
It has innocent loss and evil gain...
It has suspense and despair.
It has terrible cruelty and extreme sadness...
It has a trial and a scourging...

There is dishonour and there is valour...
There is cowardice and there is courage...
There is death and there is life...
There is grief and there is rejoicing.

What producer ever had better material to work with? Against the backdrop of Jerusalem - the Holy City - the most venerated of all cities. It is the focal point of three of the world's great religions: Judaism, Islam and Christianity; it is the most fought over city on earth.

Against this backdrop we have a kaleidoscope of scenes:

The Mount of Olives, with its unique view of the city of dreams, where Jesus wept and every tour group has its picture taken with the old city and its walls in the background...

A procession across the Kidron Valley through the ancient gates and down the narrow city streets...

A crowd scene where they strew branches and shout "Hosanna" before the approaching hero...

The great and wonderful temple on Zion's hill and a man running amok with a whip, upsetting tables and turning loose livestock...

A scene in the Temple courtyard and a man prophesying that this beautiful temple, the pride of all Israel, will be razed to the ground...

The gathering in the Upper Room where a man has his last supper with his friends...

A group of men singing an evening hymn under the olive trees...

A man praying in a garden and in his anguish his sweat was like drops of blood falling on the ground...

The garden is invaded by armed men guided by a traitor who betrays his best friend with a kiss...

A disciple grabbing a sword and slashing off an ear...

A man in front of the High Priest being slapped for insolence...

A gathering of servants, soldiers, onlookers, beside a brazier in a courtyard trying to keep warm and a friend who promised always to be faithful, denying vehemently that he has ever seen Jesus...

A cock crowing to mark his denial...

An innocent man before the Roman Governor being sentenced to death...

A crowd calling for the release of a murderer and the blood of an innocent man...

An official washing his hands...

A traitor grasping for thirty pieces of silver...

Roman-clad soldiers whipping a prisoner and crowning him with thorns...

A man carrying his own instrument of execution through crowded streets...

A farmer visiting the city being cashiered into carrying the cross...

The sickening thrum of a hammer driving spikes through flesh into timber...

A skull-shaped hill outside a city wall now crowned with three crosses bearing three dying men...

Roman soldiers throwing dice for the clothes of the dying man...

A mother and others who loved the condemned man huddled together witnessing his agony...

The darkness at noon followed by an earthquake and the ripping of the veil in the temple...

A rich man claiming the body and laying it in a borrowed tomb...

The scenes of Holy Week. All of it high drama. No script writer could match it. The variety of settings, the plot, the actors, the kaleidoscope of scenes, and the portrayal of every emotion of which humans are capable. The drama that encompasses all of life's experiences. Hollywood could not ask for more except – *except* - a more graphic ending. Surely even the most novice of script writers could have come up with something better than Mark's version: three frightened women running away from a hole in the wall containing discarded grave clothes.

I can just imagine a producer reading the manuscript with growing excitement then coming to the end and wondering, "What happened?" Did the writer die and leave an unfinished manuscript? Seeing it's an old story written on papyrus, was the ending lost?

Indeed, at least two scribes in the early Church found the ending of Mark's gospel sadly lacking and added a bit to complete it. Anyone who could write the scenario for Holy Week could surely have come up with a better ending than this. A series of events like these which were to shape the faith and lives of millions should surely culminate in a scene so glorious that it would be etched indelibly in the memory of humankind - some great scene of the triumphant Christ wearing his kingly crown blasting off into space to the glorious sounds of the Hallelujah Chorus.

The Moslems do far better for central to the Dome of the Rock, that magnificent, ageless, edifice crowning the Temple Mount, is the crown of Mount Moriah bearing an indentation which the devout Moslem will claim is the footprint of Mohammed, left there when he launched himself from that rock to heaven. Now there is an ending that is sheer Hollywood. But for the Christian, there is only a hole in the side of a hill.

It's anticlimactic like an engrossing movie that ends abruptly leaving you hanging. Mind you some Christian denominations, such as the Copts, Armenians, Syrians, Latin Catholics, Greek Orthodox and Ethiopians, maintain and constantly fight over the great Church of the Holy Sepulcher that was built over what many think was Calvary's hill and the empty tomb. But, alas, the ornate covering added in the last century - with all its lamps, ornaments and gewgaws, whose intention it is to enhance and beautify - is so crass that it leaves the visitor cold.

Far more appropriate is the most recently discovered rich man's garden and tomb outside the city wall. Far removed from the hubbub of the city we can sit beneath the olive trees and meditate before that gaping hole with the scull shaped hill in the background.

For that is all we have.

Just as the Christmas story with its variety of scenes and characters; with its magic, mystery, and suspense and that great drama and series of events that build towards the event that would fulfill the expectations of the ages...

The heralded coming of God's messiah...

The event that would bring shepherds hurrying in from their fields...

That would anger a king...

That would lead wise men from foreign lands on a journey that would end with...

What? A tiny baby in a stable. What an anticlimax! What a wonderful, perfect anticlimax.

A baby lying in a manger.

There is a wonderful moment in the history of the Temple in Jerusalem when Titus, the Roman General, stood before the Holy of Holies:

> *The year is A.D. 70 and the Romans have decided to put down the Jewish insurrection once and for all. The battle for Jerusalem was fierce. The Jews fought a determined rear guard action as they withdrew street after street, dying for every inch they gave up.*

> *Finally after an appalling slaughter the Roman General was able to enter the Temple and stand where no Gentile had ever stood before. In front of him was the curtain dividing off the Inner Sanctum, a place so holy it was entered only once a year by a priest who had been selected by drawing lots. A rope was tied around the priest's waist lest were he to become ill or faint he could be dragged out, for no man could enter to rescue him. Even today, an Orthodox Jew will not walk on the Temple Mount lest inadvertently he walk on the Holy of Holies somewhere beneath centuries of overlay.*

"Now," thought Titus, "I will find out what is in this place, this focal point of the worship of the Jews, this place so revered that no man can enter, this place so holy that the Jews are willing to die in the thousands to defend it."

Taking his sword, he slashes the curtain, allowing the sun to shine where it had never shone before. What stood before him was an empty room.

There was nothing there, absolutely nothing!

How anticlimactic… and how appropriate. In the words of King Solomon on the day when he was dedicating the glorious temple he had built as the first house of God:

"But will God indeed dwell on earth? Heaven itself and the highest heaven cannot contain Thee how much less this house that I have built." ~2 Chronicles 6:18

Sometimes like Solomon, we'd like to build a house for God. A place where we could visit him and meet him face to face, but all we have is an empty grave. And Jesus! No, he didn't take off like a rocket to somewhere in the sky. The disciples found him where they had always known him, in their relationships, in their fellowship, in the breaking of the bread, in acts of love and kindness. They discovered that he lived in them and that his power was within them…

They discovered what he had been teaching them about the healing power of love.

They discovered that Jesus lived in their hearts, the only temple worthy of his presence…

They discovered that with his help they could turn all their good Fridays into Easter…

They discovered that when they lived in love, God lived in them, and they in God…

It was like being born all over again. And what happened that first Easter, after all the pathos and cruelty and suffering of that awful Good Friday, has kept happening to God's people ever since. No matter what our pain, our fears, our depressions, our anxieties, our God is an ever present help to redeem us from our suffering and make life altogether new.

If our Easters and Christmases are anticlimactic could it be, that like Solomon at the dedication of the Temple, that we have a conception of God in some far off heaven ruling the earth like a powerful potentate ordering the devastation and destruction of entire nations while serving and protecting others?

A God all powerful, omnipotent, awesome in majesty and terrifying in anger?

A God truly to be feared?

A God who assumes authority in all our lives controlling us like puppets?

But will God indeed dwell on Earth? Yes! God did dwell on Earth, but not in the magnificent temple, nor in an ornate palace but in a stable... and his power - his awesome power - is that of a little baby, the power of the child to captivate the human heart.

> *"Thou didst leave Thy throne*
> *And Thy kingly crown*
> *When Thou camest to earth for me,*
> *But in Bethlehem's home*
> *There was found no room*
> *For Thy holy nativity:*
> *O come to my heart, Lord Jesus;*
> *There is room in my heart for Thee!*
>
> *Heaven's arches rang*
> *When the angels sang,*
> *Proclaiming Thy royal degree;*
> *But of lowly birth*
> *Camest Thou, Lord, on earth,*
> *And in great humility:*
> *O come to my heart, Lord Jesus;*
> *there is room i my heart for Thee!"*

God at Christmas reveals that his power is love and his dwelling place is in the hearts of men and women.

But then:

> *"Thou camest, O Lord;*
> *With the living word,*
> *That should set Thy people free;*
> *But, with, mocking scorn,*
> *And with crown of thorn,*
> *They bore Thee to Calvary:*
> *O come to my heart, Lord Jesus;*
> *Thy cross is my only plea!"*

The suffering of Jesus and the empty tomb was hard for the disciples to accept until they had experienced the Risen Lord in their midst. Now they knew where the dwelling place of God is: in the hearts and lives of those who love him and do his work by loving one another.

As John wrote:

> *"Behold the dwelling place of God is with men. He will dwell with them, and they shall be his people, and God himself will be with them; he will wipe away every tear from their eyes, and death shall be no more, neither shall there be mourning nor crying nor pain any more, for the former things have passed away." ~ Revelations 21:3*

> *"When heaven's arches shall ring,*
> *And her choirs shall sing*
> *At Thy coming to victory,*
> *Let Thy voice call me home,*
> *Saying, 'Yet there is room -*
> *There is room at my side for thee!'*
> *And my heart shall rejoice, Lord Jesus,*
> *When Thou comest and dwellest in me."*

Something Stirred

"And now in age I bud again;
after so many deaths I live and write;
I once more smell the dew and rain,
And relish versing. O my only Light, it cannot be
That I am he
On whom thy tempests fell all night.
These are Thy wonders, Lord of love."

~George Herbert

"He's back in the land of the living."

~Fred Kaan

Once, while driving from Calgary to Waterton United Church for our Easter celebration, I heard Brian Leaming on The Home Stretch, on CBC radio, talking to Jeff Collins about collectables he has that bring back childhood memories.

Brian talked about a boat he played with as a child, and that now sits on his coffee table. It was made by his grandfather who was an immigrant from Russia. As he talked I could hear his nostalgia for that grand old man who was such an influence on him.

All of us bring from the past scenes filled with nostalgia. Memories so full of emotion that the passing of time does little to diminish them and each time we recall them we experience once again the joy and contentment of the moment.

For me the memory that surfaced from my childhood was that of being in school at the age of ten and hearing my favourite teacher read the words, *Down in the hedgerow something stirred...* This would happen at the end of the week if the class had completed its work. She would read a story beginning with, "Down in the hedgerow something stirred..."

I can remember sitting silently at my desk on a warm summer afternoon while the slanting sunbeams held in their rays tiny particles of dust and lint suspended in the still air.

"Down in the hedgerow something stirred...", she would begin, or, "Down in the meadow something stirred...", or, "Down in the forest something stirred...", and the story would tell about the emergence of the badger from his burrow into the spring sunshine, or the return of a pair of swallows to nest in the eaves of the barn after their migration south, or the snake shedding his old skin, or the pair of foxes with new kits frolicking around the mouth of their den. Yes, down in the hedgerow something stirred- heralding a new day - a new beginning, a new season, a new generation, or a new challenge.

Easter is the time of the year when we are all aware that things are stirring. After the dead of winter new life is beginning to stir; the sap is flowing in the trees and the pussy willows are budding. The ice has gone from the river and again the water is flowing. In the lifeless brown grass green shoots are appearing, and through the hard earth of the coulees crocuses are breaking through and tulips are beginning to emerge from their long winter's sleep.

We sense new life stirring all around. Even without seeing it we feel it and the symbolism of spring is a counterpart of that newness of life we seek within ourselves. For deep, deep within us, something is stirring,

Something is unsettling us in the midst of our contentment...

Something is upsetting us in the midst of our complacency...

Something is stirring - something deep within us - calling us forth to be the people God intended us to be.

It's the Divine Discontent: God prodding us, motivating us, unsettling us and stirring us out of our long sleep of lethargy to a life of new beginnings.

On a spring morning, long, long ago, just as the day was dawning in an eastern city, down in the garden something was stirring. Predictably, in the heart of a busy city - especially one thronged with pilgrims from far and wide converging to celebrate the Passover early in the morning - many things would be astir…

Early pilgrims on their ascent to the temple on Zion's hill…

The High Priests on their way to their morning devotions…

Women on their way to the Pool of Siloam to draw the day's supply of water….

Beggars moving to stake out the choice locations at the Temple Gate…

Merchants hurrying to catch the early tourist…

Soldiers, the narrow streets ringing with the tramp of their boots, on their way to relieve their colleagues who had been on watch all night at the tomb of the man they had crucified…

Some women, dressed in the rags of mourning, making their way to the tomb of Joseph of Arimathea to anoint the body of their dead companion.

Yes, dawn's early light saw much expected movement in the Holy City, predictably so, but down in the garden something stirred, something not expected to move - not ever. Down in the garden the boulder that sealed the entrance to the tomb had stirred. It had moved. The mouth of the burial cave was agape and the body had stirred. It was gone leaving only the grave clothes in the empty tomb.

It boggled the imagination. It defied comprehension. And yet, there it was. Down in the garden something stirred. The boulder was rolled away and Jesus, this friend of friends;

this man in whose presence life had taken on a new dimension;

this companion, in whose company life had become totally different;

this teacher, in whose audience, life's mysteries had become clear;

this healer, by whose touch people had become whole;

this Master, in whose presence the yoke had become easy and the burden light;

this friend, whom they had loved and lost awhile, had left the grave, the stone had been rolled away and the burial tomb was empty.

What did it all mean?

For the disciples, once they had recovered from their confusion, guilt, and fear, it was the beginning of a new day. Jesus. Their Jesus, was not a lifeless body hauled down from a cross and sealed in a tomb, but a living presence standing in their midst empowering them to fulfill their mandate and go forth into that pagan world - that oppressive, demeaning, hurting world - and liberate the captives by the power of the Gospel. And that tottering, sordid, sad, hopeless old world experienced a new day as a new voice burst forth out of Palestine with the shout, "*Christ is risen, he has risen indeed*".

Down in the garden something stirred; the stone has been rolled away.

There's a stone in Greek Mythology that describes the lives of many in that pre-Easter world. And it describes all too many in our world today. It is the boulder that Sisyphus was condemned to spend eternity pushing up a hill and every time he almost succeeded in reaching the top it slipped from his grasp and rolled to the foot and the long painful struggle would begin all over again.

The law of the Jews was like that. It was, or had become, a terrible burden on the people. The fulfilling of the law, with its myriads of interpretations, was a wearisome business and the goal of God's kingdom on earth - which would come, some believed - when every Jew fulfilled the requirements of the law for one whole day. It was still a faraway dream.

It hadn't always been like that. When the despised Babylonians in the face of the advancing army of invaders had to load their gods onto the back of their animals, Isaiah, the Prophet, had a heyday scoffing at them.

"*Look at them*", he jeered, "*their gods are a burden to them*", they have to carry them, they are a dead weight".

How unlike the God of Israel, our God, who bears us up and carries us. In his immortal words Isaiah, God's spokesman records,

> "*Hearken to me, you who have been borne by me since your birth, even when you are old and your hair is grey I will carry you. I have made you, and I will support you, I will carry you, and I will save you*". ~Isaiah 46:3

No, our God is not a burden on our backs but is the wind beneath our wings. But by the time of Jesus the religion of the Temple has fossilized; it is a burden on the backs of the people, an unending endeavour to be right with God through the fulfilling of the law and temple sacrifices.

No more says Jesus. It is the heart that counts and not the ritual. The way we respond to the needy, the poor, the captives, the dispossessed, is the true worship. It is love that unites us with God's kingdom and not the fulfilling of the law. God's love is unconditional. It cannot be earned or deserved; it is freely given.

No longer do people need to work for approval…

No longer do we need to perform for acceptance…

No longer do we need to please people for them to like us…

No longer do we need to strive for perfection and be fearful of failure…

No longer do we need to be a certain shape, or size, or attain a certain standard of fitness to be accepted…

No longer do need to fill our hours with business and work to be of worth…

No longer do we have to be good in order to be loved.

Modern psychology has identified all of the above as Adaptive behaviours which are a compromise of our true selves. They are the projections of childhood when we decided that to be loved by our care givers we had to be a certain way, behave a certain way, live a certain way, and the payoff - when we fail, and fail we will - is to be depressed, fearful, inadequate, anxious, angry, sad, disillusioned and feel abandoned and worthless. These are the burdens that rob us of the joy of living.

If you are fed up with your heavy load,

if you want to be free of your pain,

if you want to get out from under,

if your burden is too heavy, you may be experiencing the Divine Discontent, the restlessness of God letting us know that we were not created for slavery and our hearts are restless till they find rest in him.

Jesus said,

"Come to me all who labour and are heavy laden and I will give you rest. Take my yoke upon you, and learn from me; for I am gentle and lowly in heart, and you will find rest for your souls.

For my yoke is easy, and my burden is light". ~Matthew 11:28-30

My definition of sinfulness is; *Our striving to be who we think we are supposed to be, in order to be right with God, instead of being the person God created us to be.*

Jesus teaches that God's love is without condition -there is nothing we need to do or be

to deserve it. The burden of the law has been lifted, no longer is salvation earned; it is God's free gift to his children, we are saved by faith and faith alone.

Down in the garden something stirred…, something that shouldn't have moved, a large stone designed to seal off the dead from the living, and this Jesus - this reformer, this radical, this upstart who defied the law, this man who challenged the authority of the high priests of the old time religion was safely behind it - they had killed him. He was dead. He was gone. He was finished, but down in the garden something stirred… The stone had moved the tomb couldn't contain him, and he was standing in the midst of his disciples empowering them once more as he empowers each and every one of us.

He's back in the land of the living,
the man we decided to kill;
he's standing among us, forgiving
our guilt on Good Friday hill.
He calls us to share in his rising,
to abandon the grave of our past;
he offers us present and future,
a world that is open and vast.

~Fred Kaan.

~The End~

About the Author

Alex Lawson is a coal miner become minister. He was born in Scotland and came to Canada to play the bagpipes. He graduated from McGill University in Montreal and was ordained into the ministry of The United Church of Canada. He and his wife, Joy, have been married for 57 years. They have six children and eleven grand children.